SAS AND ELITE FORCES GUIDE
EXTREME
UNARMED

MW00640031

SAS AND ELITE FORCES GUIDE
EXTREME UNARMED COMBAT

HAND-TO-HAND FIGHTING SKILLS
FROM THE WORLD'S ELITE MILITARY UNITS

MARTIN J. DOUGHERTY

LYONS PRESS
Guilford, Connecticut

An imprint of Globe Pequot Press

Copyright © 2012 Amber Books Ltd
All illustrations © Amber Books Ltd
Published by Amber Books Ltd (www.amberbooks.co.uk)

This Lyons Press edition first published in 2012

Lyons Press is an imprint of Globe Pequot Press.

Library of Congress Cataloging-in-Publication Data is available on file.

ISBN: 978-0-7627-7990-1

Project Editor: Michael Spilling
Designer: Rajdip Sanghera
Illustrations: Tony Randell

Printed in Singapore

10 9 8 7 6 5 4 3 2 1

CONTENTS

INTRODUCTION

Military, security and law enforcement personnel operate in an environment where extreme violence can erupt at any time. They often carry weapons, but weapons can be dropped, malfunction or run out of ammunition. When all else fails, unarmed combat skills can make all the difference.

The average police officer operating in a civilized area is less likely to encounter extreme violence than a soldier in a war zone, so for the most part we will consider military skills and applications. However, specialist police units such as hostage-rescue or Special Weapons and Tactics (SWAT), anti-terrorist police and also those operating in unstable regions may well need to make use of the same kind of skills.

Police work can be dangerous, of course, and his uniform can make an officer the target for a level of deliberate violence not normally encountered by civilians. In this situation the officer may be fighting to survive rather than to arrest a suspect and, if so, may have recourse to some of the more aggressive skills in this book.

Law Enforcement

The line between 'combat' and 'law enforcement' unarmed combat skills

If suddenly attacked in close urban terrain a soldier's 'unarmed' combat skills may be vital in creating space to use his weapon. His unarmed combat training also builds confidence and fighting spirit.

is a blurry one at best. For example, Eric A. Sykes and William E. Fairbairn developed a system called Defendu, which is used as the basis of many modern unarmed combat systems. Defendu drew on experience gained in policing rather than military applications, but was then developed into a system to be taught to commandos and secret agents during World War II.

The similarly-named Defendo system was developed by Bill Underwood after World War II. His original system, named Combato, was an open-hand 'combatives' system for military applications and was extremely lethal. When asked to teach this system to law enforcement agencies after the war, Underwood instead modified it to create Defendo, which was less aggressive and better tailored to law enforcement requirements. Many elements were exactly the same in both systems.

Similarly the martial art of Krav Maga was developed as a result of its creator's experiences fighting against Fascist gangs in the 1930s and was adopted by the Israeli armed forces. Variants have since been created for military, police and self-defence applications, all of which use the same basic techniques and concepts.

Depending on the circumstances, unarmed combat skills may be all that a soldier or police officer has at his disposal. They may also be used alongside a weapon. For example, a police officer may choose to employ his unarmed skills so that he does not have to use his weapon, and a soldier may have to use his combat skills in order to retain his weapon. This represents both sides of the same coin; unarmed combat skills give personnel an increased range of capabilities, and they are there when there are no other options.

Given all the other skills that police and military personnel must master, there is little time for training in complex martial arts systems. Some personnel do train in formal martial arts on their own time, but given that hand-to-hand combat is not the primary function of soldiers or police officers, the time available for 'official' training is strictly limited.

Thus military and police combat systems are a backup to other skills. They must be quick to learn and simple to use, yet effective under very difficult conditions. Whatever label is used – arrest and restraint, officer safety, close-quarters battle, combatives or hand-to-hand combat – the same factors apply. The system has to work quickly and completely; the opponent must be neutralized as fast as possible. Any other outcome can lead to disaster.

For most civilians, losing a fight can mean taking a beating, which is bad enough. For those who operate in a more extreme

Law Enforcement Tip: It's Not Like The Movies!

A real fight is never like a choreographed movie scene or martial arts sparring. It will always be a chaotic scramble; frightening, painful and desperate. Police officers and soldiers are trained to accept the reality that a win is a win, even if it looks like a scruffy mess.

environment, defeat means death or capture. It can also lead to a failed mission and friendly casualties. Thus although unarmed combat is not the primary role of soldiers and police officers, they must be ready when it happens.

Mixed Martial Arts (MMA) training is geared to a fair one-on-one fight with rules and a referee. It is, however, an excellent way to develop combat skills for any situation.

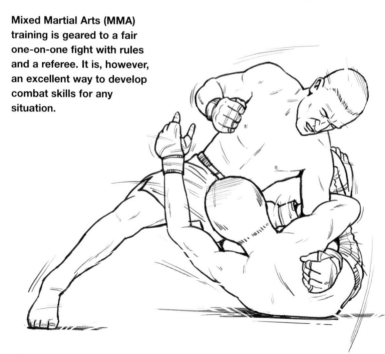

Martial Arts vs Unarmed Combat

It is impossible to say exactly when the term 'martial arts' was coined. Originally it meant something like 'fighting skills' and referred to life-or-death close combat. However, in the modern age the term has come to refer to a wide range of activities, some of them only vaguely connected with combat.

Some modern martial arts are useless for fighting. That does not make them worthless of course; they simply have other virtues and are often a worthy athletic endeavour in their own right. However, for those going in harm's way as part of their occupational duties, these arts are of little value.

Other arts are more practical and often have real value in unarmed combat. However, it takes time to learn a martial art to the standard where it is useful in a fight, and along the way there are many hours spent learning skills that will never be used.

It requires long training to be able to make high kicks work in combat. For most personnel the time is better spent on other, less flashy, skills.

Special Forces Tip: The Red Light

Many military systems work on the concept of an imaginary 'red light'. When the red light comes on it's GO! GO! GO! until the threat is neutralized. The soldier must decide beforehand what will make the red light come on. It might be seeing an opponent's fists come up or him reaching for a weapon, or it might be an order from a superior. Whatever the trigger, once the red light is on then the violence does not stop until the enemy is down and out of the fight.

For example, a sport martial artist will need to learn how to escape from a range of submission holds that a soldier on the battlefield is extremely unlikely to encounter.

With limited time available for training, the soldier needs to learn to deal with the most likely situations and to demolish his opponent fast rather than rolling around the floor for 10 minutes trying to apply an armlock. The converse is also true. A soldier or police officer trained in 'quick and dirty' unarmed combat methods would probably be defeated in a formal match with a trained mixed martial artist, kickboxer or judo player. Such a situation is beyond his area of expertise.

The fundamental difference between martial arts and unarmed combat training is that unarmed combat is 100 per cent geared towards the destruction or neutralization of the opponent. Restraints might be taught as part of an arrest and restraint package, but for the most part military personnel are trained to destroy their opponent, not merely defeat him.

Where a martial artist might learn complex counters to an opponent's martial arts techniques, the unarmed combat practitioner learns simple moves that will do maximum damage to the target. Not only is there little time for anything else, this is actually the most effective skill set. In an extreme environment, extreme measures are the key to victory.

Elements of military and law enforcement unarmed combat skills are highly useful for civilian self-defence. While the more extreme

Simple escapes from adverse situations, such as the 'mount' are a useful part of unarmed combat training. There is neither the time nor the need to get into the complexities of advanced groundfighting.

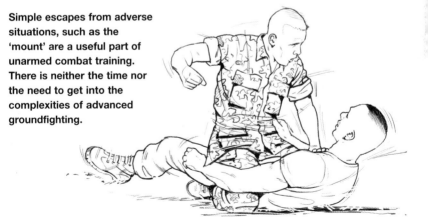

measures are not appropriate in most situations, a self-defence system drawn from military and police experience has much to recommend it. Not everyone has the time to study a martial art to a high level, and not all martial arts are effective for self-defence.

Military Systems

For someone who wants to achieve an effective level of self-defence capability without putting in endless hours, the military systems offer an indication of what works in a fight, and what can be quickly learned. This has led to the formulation of martial arts based around military principles. For example, the martial art of Krav Maga, based on the unarmed combat system of the Israeli armed forces, has recently become very popular worldwide.

There are also self-defence systems that draw on military and security experience. The Modern Street Combat system taught by the Self Defence Federation is not a martial art as such; it is instead a pure self-defence system drawing on aspects of military combative systems, martial arts such as ju-jitsu and traditional western fighting systems such as Catch Wrestling.

Conversely, elements of some martial arts are used by military and law enforcement personnel. Aikido and ju-jitsu are often used as the basis for arrest & restraint training as

they have excellent joint-locking techniques. Other martial arts are used by the military for training purposes. For example, Brazilian Jiu-Jitsu (BJJ) is used by the US military.

This is not because soldiers are expected to roll around on the ground with Taliban fighters trying to get a submission hold; that would be ridiculous. However, training in a competitive grappling system like BJJ allows soldiers to engage in a safe but extremely demanding sport that builds confidence and fighting spirit as well as being a hard workout. The benefits in terms of confidence and offensive mind-set are immense, even though the skills themselves are not all that applicable to the battlefield.

Thus some martial arts are of use to the military even if their specific skills will not be used. Others can be plundered for their most useful techniques or concepts. But when it comes to training soldiers to fight, martial arts are put aside in favour of a quick-and-dirty fighting system that relies on a few simple moves done with guts and determination.

Military and Security Applications

Slightly different skill sets are necessary depending on the situation. Security professionals (e.g. doormen and bodyguards) and police officers often need to get control of a person without doing them much harm, and have to remain within legal limits while doing so. Military personnel attempting to capture a prisoner for interrogation or who are using a low-level response to a threat may also make use of control and restraint techniques. This might happen when protecting an installation from an intruder who might turn out to be fairly harmless, or when deployed on a peacekeeping mission.

On the other hand, any of these personnel can be savagely attacked in the course of their duties. In the event of a lethal threat, extreme measures are justified. A police officer who loses his weapon in a struggle with a suspect and thinks the assailant is going to try to use it against him, or a soldier whose rifle jams in a close-quarters urban battle, needs to make an overwhelmingly effective response to the situation. There can be no half measures in this environment; often it is literally kill or be killed.

If a suspect suddenly begins resisting whilst being handcuffed, the officer is placed in a dangerous situation where he may not have time or space to deploy his weapon.

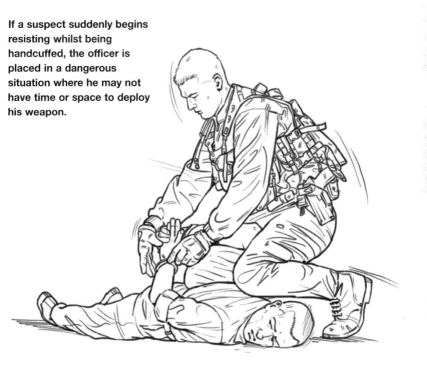

Bodyguard Tip: What's Going On?

It is impossible to respond effectively to a situation without information. That means keeping alert and watching for anything out of the ordinary. Violence can explode at any time, but good situational awareness will give you enough warning to deal with it.

Special Forces Tip: It Ain't Pretty

Military personnel are trained to take the best opportunity that presents itself and to attack whenever possible. There is no time for elegant technique or subtle countermoves. The aim is to demolish the enemy, not dance with them.

A number of stripped-down civilian self-defence systems exist, which apply the principles of military unarmed combat. Whilst care must be taken not to use excessive measures, the civilian who is facing a brutal beating by a gang, or who is attacked with the intent to cause death or severe harm, needs to be able to respond at an appropriate level. Effective self-defence training (as opposed to martial arts) is not very different to the military unarmed combat systems. Quick and dirty, simple and effective – that's what works in an extreme situation.

Legal Matters

As previously noted, sometimes it is necessary for military and law enforcement personnel to limit the level of force they use in order to remain within the law. This applies even more so to civilian security operatives and private citizens who might need to defend themselves. The law permits anyone who fears for his safety to use reasonable and necessary force to protect himself.

The situation is not enormously different in a war zone. Soldiers are bound by international law and will answer for unlawful actions. The main difference is the sort of situation they are likely to encounter. Obviously, when fighting a declared enemy who is armed with automatic weapons, grenades and possibly artillery responding in kind is appropriate. In any situation where a soldier would be justified in firing his weapon, any unarmed combat move is certainly lawful.

Soldiers operating in a combat zone are not merely entitled to engage the enemy with whatever means they have at their disposal, they are usually required to do so unless it compromises a more important mission. This includes lethal force. In civilian life, someone who rendered an opponent helpless and then stamped on their head or choked them to death would probably be prosecuted for murder, but in a war

15

Law Enforcement Tip: Keeping Control

Most aggressors will only attack if they think the odds are good. Police officers are trained to control a situation so that a potential assailant does not get too close or move around behind them where they can attack on their own terms. Maintaining good awareness of the situation is essential to avoid being blindsided. Tactical mobility, changing position to keep potential assailants within the frontal arc, is an effective tool, but it is also possible to use obstructions to limit the opponents' options. Police officers will also issue commands, such as, 'Do not attempt to go behind me!' or 'Stay there!' This not only asserts dominance over the situation but also informs the potential assailant that the officer knows exactly what he is up to.

zone finishing off an opponent is often acceptable. Indeed, it may be necessary to the mission or to the survival of friendly troops. A hostile who can get back up and attack again is a continued threat that cannot be accepted.

Nor need the soldier worry too much about his level of force. If an enemy is trying to restrain the soldier to take him prisoner, or is trying to make an unarmed attack against an armed soldier, this makes little difference. What matters is that the target must be identified as a declared enemy whom the soldier has permission to operate against, and the soldier's actions must not contravene international law. Executing enemy wounded or prisoners is murder, even in a war zone, but killing a sentry to prevent him raising the alarm is a necessary part of warmaking.

In short, military personnel are subject to 'rules of engagement', which dictate what targets can be engaged and in what circumstances. These rules apply whether the soldier is calling in an airstrike or engaging in unarmed combat. Decisions about whether or not to engage are made before the fight begins, possibly by the other side in the event that they initiate an attack. Either way, once in contact with an enemy who is determined to kill him, all the soldier needs to worry about is winning the fight.

Surrendering property in return for not being cut or stabbed is a reasonably good outcome. However, if the assailant tries to use the weapon, or attempts to abduct his victim, then the only option is to fight. A knife attack justifies extreme measures; anything less will fail, with fatal consequences.

PART ONE: TOOLS

For most people, the possibility of encountering violence in their daily lives is remote. Crimes are committed of course, and disputes can escalate, but in most cases if we do not go looking for trouble, it is fairly unlikely to find us.

The chief reason for this is that there are those who are willing to go looking for trouble on our behalf. Soldiers may be sent to a conflict zone, or have to fight to protect our nation. Police officers will respond to an emergency call. These people voluntarily go in harm's way to protect others. It is only right, then, that have at their disposal a suitable set of tools.

Many of those tools are physical, for example, firearms, body armour and communications equipment. Opposition will often surrender or melt away when shots are fired, or when it becomes obvious that armed force is about to be used. But there are other tools at the disposal of a soldier or police officer. Most of the time they cannot be seen, but they are there when there is nothing else. And that can make all the difference.

When extreme violence erupts, you fight with what you have. In the case of a soldier in a war zone that can mean a rifle or machine gun, grenades, a bayonet and an assortment of heavy pieces of equipment that can be used to bash an opponent. Improvised weapons can be grabbed from the ground or the surroundings – it is possible to do a lot of damage with a rock, a stick, a spanner or a fire extinguisher.

However, sometimes a soldier will be thrown back on his own resources and must use his body for both attack and defence. This can happen for all kinds of reasons, for example, if hostiles have infiltrated a supposedly secure area to try to take a hostage or prisoner, or weapons might be dropped in close-quarters battle. With no time to arm himself properly, the soldier fights as he stands.

So what does he have at his disposal? What tools does the unarmed soldier or disarmed police officer have to save himself from attack? If he has been properly trained, he will have some lethal skills at his disposal and, more importantly, the will to use them.

. . . .

A good 'ready stance' is a starting point from which to move, defend or attack. It is extremely important to set yourself correctly – No Stance: No Chance.

1

Huge buildings are constructed on firm foundations. In the same way, a good set of combat skills requires a sound grasp of the basics.

Basics

Vulnerable Points

A soldier's equipment may get in his way during unarmed combat, but it also greatly reduces the options available to an attacker. Body armour will stop or at least mitigate most blows, and there is no point at all in striking a helmet or a loaded rifle magazine.

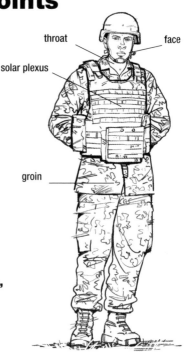

Military combat systems must take into account both the encumbering nature of standard equipment and the lack of available targets. The face, throat and groin are all still accessible and are preferred targets for military unarmed combat. Not coincidentally, these are also some of the most vulnerable parts of a human being.

It is also possible to kick the legs or to try to break an arm, or to throw the opponent into the ground hard enough that he is injured by the fall. A downed opponent can also be finished off with the boots and, as a general rule, protection such as body armour is much less effective when a soldier is flat on his back being stomped on. A primary goal of most unarmed combat systems is to avoid this happening.

Special Forces Tip: Fight on your Own Terms

Special forces units are almost always outnumbered. They win by keeping the enemy off balance and confused. They fight on their own terms, not those of the enemy.

Principles of Unarmed Combat

The key principle of unarmed combat is the intent to do as much damage to the opponent as possible in the shortest time. There is no room for fair play, and dirty tricks are in no way dishonourable. Indeed, they represent a shortcut to victory and possibly the only chance of survival.

The most important thing a soldier takes into combat is a will to win and a willingness to hurt the opponent. He may not want harm anyone – most people, soldiers included, do not actually like causing suffering to others – but what he wants is irrelevant. What matters is what he must do in order to survive. Facing an enemy who is willing (and perhaps even eager) to kill him, the soldier must respond with the same level of aggression and violence or perish.

The combat skills an individual has, coupled with his strength, fitness and sense of tactics, are all tools that can be used to good advantage. They are, however, entirely worthless without a guiding will. A soldier who

hesitates to strike a killing blow or panics in the face of extreme aggression is likely to lose. Thus military training fosters an aggressive mind-set, enabling the soldier to put aside other concerns and get the job done. It is this ability to get stuck in and dish out damage that will carry the soldier through a desperate situation.

In short, everything else depends on a willingness to fight.

Attack: the Best Form of Defence

As a general rule, being on the defensive leads to defeat. Martial artists and sport fighters can afford to play a subtle and clever game, drawing the opponent into making a mistake. A soldier has no time for that, even if it is likely to work. Instead he will take every opportunity to attack, overwhelming the opponent before he can act or help can arrive.

If he is aggressive enough, the soldier may not have to defend at all. Even facing multiple opponents, if he

23

Special Forces Tip: Defence

Defence is what you have to do when you screw up. If you're being attacked then you're not fighting on your own terms, you're allowing the opponent to dictate what's happening. That's bad.

keeps moving and attacking he may confound their attempts to launch attacks of their own without actually defending as such.

Any defence that is made must serve two purposes. Firstly, it must defeat whatever attack is incoming or at least mitigate it sufficiently that the soldier can survive it. He may be in pain or even need medical attention afterwards, but if he has defeated an opponent intent on killing him then that's a win. Secondly, defence should not be purely defensive. Dodging a blow is of little value if the soldier gets hit again a second later, but dodging a blow and landing one of his own is a step towards victory.

Obviously, some defensive measures are necessary or the soldier will be taken out of the fight by anyone who succeeds in launching an attack of any sort, but the soldier must use an aggressive offensive-defence as much as possible and if he is forced entirely on the defensive (for example he is grabbed and held) then he must find a way to retake the initiative as fast as possible.

Stance and Movement

Many martial arts are excessively concerned about 'stances', many of which are unnatural and/or limiting in various ways. Whilst probably useful within their own environment, stylised martial arts stances are irrelevant to extreme situations. You do not win by standing around in an impressive stance; you win by doing something.

Most unarmed combat systems teach a basic 'ready' stance or guard position, but that's all it is – a starting point. Once a fight starts the soldier needs to be moving constantly, aggressively advancing on his opponent and taking him out of the fight before moving on to the next target. A guard or ready stance is just a position you pass through on the way to doing something useful; it is not an end to itself.

The basic ready stance is not unlike a boxer's guard. The strong hand (usually right) is kept back whilst the weaker one is advanced slightly. Hands are up and usually open rather than being balled into fists as this gives a greater range of

Ready Stance

If violence erupts then the soldier will not spend much time in a ready stance – he will be far too busy attacking, moving or defending. Thus there are no points to be scored for a perfect 'fighting stance'. All that is necessary is for the soldier to be able to launch powerful strikes, to avoid being hit or grabbed, and to move around freely.

Hands can be loosely curled or held as fists; it does not matter all that much so long as they are up and ready to strike or defend the head. Normally the strong hand is kept back and the weaker hand (usually the left) is advanced. This soldier may be left-handed, or may have switched to a

'Southpaw' or 'Opposite-Lead' stance for tactical reasons.

options. Elbows are held in close to the ribs for protection. The body is turned at about 45 degrees to protect the internal organs. Feet will also be turned in slightly, with knees flexed ready to move. From this position the

soldier can move in any direction and turn to face new threats.

Keep Moving
Movement is the key to success and survival in battle. Constant movement

The Shuffle

Normally, we cross our feet when we walk, but this can make a soldier very vulnerable. If he is attacked in mid-stride he will not be able to react immediately, and his balance will be compromised. Most combat movement uses a 'shuffle' for this reason. A shuffle maintains the same lead, i.e. if the left hand is forward, it remains so.

Rather than stepping normally, the soldier pushes off with his back foot (B) and advances his lead foot, then brings his back foot up so that his feet are once again about shoulder width apart (C). Going backwards is the opposite; the front foot drives the motion and the back foot makes the step.

A

B

C

makes the soldier a difficult target for unarmed attacks or anyone trying to shoot at him. It is important to move fast but to remain well balanced to launch an attack, so often a 'shuffle' style of movement is used. This maintains the guard position and avoids compromising balance by crossing the feet.

The basic principle of the shuffle is that it is all about pushing rather than stepping. To move forwards, the soldier drives himself with his back foot and lifts the front one just enough to make the step. Then he brings up his back foot so that his feet are once again about shoulder-width apart.

Backwards is the opposite; the soldier drives himself backwards with his front foot (this does not work well if he stands upright with straight legs; a slightly crouched posture with flexed knees facilitates rapid movement) and steps with the back foot, then catches up with the front one.

Diagonal movement and sidestepping use the same principle; the soldier pushes himself in the direction he wants to go, then moves his foot to that location. This is the opposite of normal walking, where the lead foot steps and the body then catches up.

Sometimes a soldier will take a normal step or run if it is appropriate. He might also dive, roll or jump as necessary. There are no hard-and-fast rules for movement in combat, other than this: however the soldier moves, he must get where he is going fast and ready to attack or defend when he gets there.

Law Enforcement Tip: Seize the Initiative

Police officers are trained to take control of a situation, to act rather than reacting to what the opponent does. They decide what they want to do, and then do it, forcing the opponent to try to catch up.

Aggression and Tactics

As already noted, pure defence does not win fights. It is necessary to do harm to the opponent and desirable to do it as early in the fight as possible. An opponent who is down and out of the fight cannot attack, which means that the soldier has successfully defended against whatever he might have done.

Simply piling into the nearest enemy can be surprisingly effective, but it is generally necessary to temper aggression with judgement. Where a soldier faces multiple opponents, the nearest may not be

Bodyguard Tip: Remember What You're Trying to Do

Bodyguards are there to protect the client, not to win a fight with attackers. Fixating on one aspect of a situation can leave a dangerous hole in your capabilities, so be constantly aware of what's going on and ready to respond to a new threat.

the most dangerous or the ideal target. It may be better to shove one opponent into another, neutralizing them both for a couple of seconds, in order to gain time to destroy a third.

Striking and Grappling
Most military unarmed combat systems rely heavily on striking methods. This has some big advantages, notably that it will take an opponent out of the fight fast without entangling the soldier with his enemy. Sophisticated joint-locking techniques can be hard to apply in the middle of a fight, and the last thing a soldier needs is to find himself struggling with one opponent while another hits him from behind.

Thus 'grappling' techniques are secondary to striking techniques for all-out combat. Grappling is useful in certain circumstances, however. It can be used to control an opponent so that he can be arrested or captured, it can be used to disarm an opponent

or break his limbs, and it can be used to silently kill an enemy who has been surprised or overwhelmed.

Grappling techniques are also frequently used in conjunction with strikes. For example, an opponent can be grabbed around the head, kneed in the body and then slammed into the ground to do further damage. Not only will this cause injury but it also puts the opponent in a position where he is extremely vulnerable.

Military combat systems do not concern themselves with the highly effective but difficult throws of judo or the submission holds of ju-jitsu. Where takedowns, chokes and joint locks are used they are simple and relatively easy to apply. Soldiers cannot rely on a one-on-one fight and so must be able to deal with an opponent and then move quickly onto the next.

Striking techniques are also somewhat different to those used in sport martial arts. For one thing the soldier is likely to be operating in an environment where killing or maiming an enemy is acceptable, and so will use strikes to the eyes and throat as a preferred option rather than a last resort. Equally, opponents may well be wearing helmets or body armour, which limits striking options.

A soldier cannot afford to break bones in his hand and be unable to use his weapon, so military systems tend to make limited use of fists. Even without the risk of hitting a helmet, it is not hard to break a hand striking the head. Thus military unarmed combat tactics emphasize use of fists only to the softer parts of the body, e.g. under the ribs or the kidney area. For most other targets, other striking techniques are used. These include palm strikes, hammerfists and elbow strikes, all of which are designed to protect the hands whilst still delivering massive damage to the target.

Special Forces Tip: The Chin jab

A palm strike to the jaw, often called a 'chin jab', was the mainstay of the striking methods taught to World War II British commandos. It worked so well that they did not need much else.

Attack and Defence

The attacker has the advantage of retaining the initiative; the defender must react rather than doing what he wants to do. Generally speaking, aggression will overwhelm most opponents despite their attempts to defend, so a soldier forced onto the defensive must find a way to counterattack as soon as possible.

However, attacks must be defended. It is necessary to
neutralize or at least mitigate an attack in order to stay
in the fight. Most defences are simple; ducking or
dodging, or covering the target with a less vulnerable
body part. Defence must be used intelligently and as part
of a fight-and-win strategy. A soldier who panics and
simply covers up will, at best, just prolong the beating.

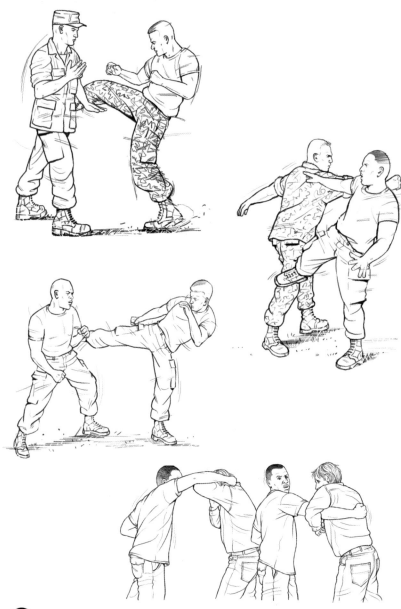

Whilst defence is not the ideal option, it is necessary in order to survive an opponent's attack and carry on with the fight. The best ways to defend against an opponent are to avoid him completely, hide from him or sneak past, or to put him on the defensive (or on the ground) with a devastating assault. If all that fails and the opponent manages to attack, then an offensive-defence still gives the soldier a chance to improve the situation.

Movement and Evasion

Movement is a basic defensive tool. By constantly being on the move, the soldier can deny his enemy a clean attack. Indeed, the opponent may not attack at all if he cannot see a good opening. Movements can be quite big, such as opening or closing the range, or fairly small, such as ducking a blow.

When close to an opponent, often the best direction to move is straight at him, covering the advance with an attack – if he is trying not to get hit, the opponent is not counterpunching. However, boring straight in can be suicidal, especially if the enemy has a

· ·

Defensive tools include evasion, covering the target and deflection of an attack. The key is to focus your defence at the weakest point of the attack rather than meeting its power head-on.

2

Pure defence does not win fights, but a good defence can be used to set up a devastating counterattack.

Defensive Tools

Evade and Counterattack

The attacker has launched a powerful but wild swinging punch at the head. This is one of the most common of all unarmed attacks and is devastating if it lands, but it is relatively easy to defeat.

The soldier ducks under the punch and steps
diagonally forwards, positioning himself for a
sideways stamping kick into the legs. His
defensive movement not only kept him safe, it
also set up the counterattack.

weapon. So the soldier will try to circle and move to the flanks. Most enemies will be right-handed and thus their most potent attacks will tend to come from that side, so moving to the opponent's left (the soldier's own right) is usually the best option.

Once in close, the number of useful movements is strictly limited. Backwards is rarely a good idea. Moving away from an opponent allows him to advance, which gives him both physical and psychological advantages. The soldier may also trip on something and, in any case, retreating does not win battles. If it is necessary to break off combat, the best way is to make an opportunity (say by striking the opponent) then make a rapid escape down a planned route. That can mean little more than deciding to flee in a certain direction, but there needs to be some objective beyond simply running blindly away. Evading towards safety is a good option; fleeing away from danger often leads to new problems.

Sidestepping and suddenly closing in are the most useful in-close movement options. If the opponent commits to an attack, say a bayonet thrust, then moving to the side takes the soldier out of danger and presents an opportunity to move in and attack. When fighting unarmed, getting close is the only option. Moving back robs the soldier of an opportunity to do anything but be a target.

The Tactical 'Y'

Many unarmed combat systems use the concept of the Tactical 'Y'. The soldier stands on the bottom leg of the Y shape. His opponent is in the crook of the Y. At this point both are equal, but if the soldier moves onto one leg of the Y, turning to face his opponent, then his weapons (e.g. kicks, strikes and blows with whatever he is holding) face the opponent while the opponent is facing empty air. While he reorientates himself the soldier can deliver telling strikes. This works best against an opponent who commits himself to an attack.

It is also possible to duck under attacks, of course. This is most effective against swinging strikes with a fist or weapon. Just ducking achieves little (other than not being hit) so the soldier moves forward and comes up on the outside of the strike. This is another use of the Tactical 'Y', positioning the soldier to counterattack.

Cover Defence

Faced with an attack that is already on its way, the soldier has few options. His best chance is to cover the area that is about to be hit and move to try to mitigate the strike somewhat. If a blow is coming in along an arc, such as a roundhouse kick or swing with a blunt weapon, then moving away from the strike can weaken it, but a better option is

The Tactical 'Y'

Wherever possible, the soldier will not stay in front of an attack where it is most powerful. Facing a charging enemy with a bayonet, this is about the worst place on Planet Earth that it is possible to be.

The soldier therefore moves off the line of attack, positioning himself on the opponent's flank where he can deliver a counterattacking blow. The upper arms of the 'Y' are good places to be; the tail is not. If the opponent reorientates himself so that the soldier is once again on the tail of the 'Y' then he must move to the flank once more.

Cover Defence 1

Against a swinging punch to the head, the defender covers by raising his arm as if trying to grab the back of his own head. As soon as the attack lands, the defender wraps the striking arm and grips it firmly. As the attacker struggles to pull his arm free, the defender launches his own counterattack.

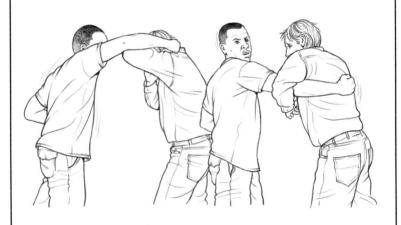

Cover Defence 2

Against a roundhouse kick to the body, the soldier weakens the attack by moving closer to the attacker or sideways, away from the strike. He covers his ribs with his arm and allows his body to flex, absorbing the kick. It will still hurt, but the soldier will now be well positioned to attack the opponent while he is still regaining his balance after the failed kick.

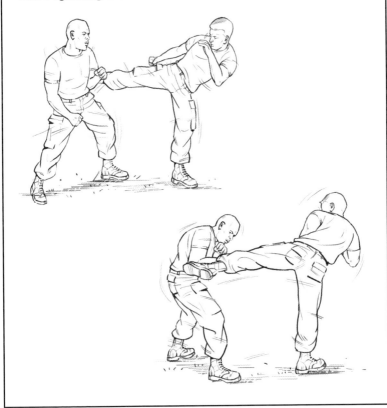

to move towards the opponent. This not only robs the blow of power but also positions the soldier for a counterattack.

Covering the head makes use of a classic 'flinch reflex' that all humans have when threatened, bringing the arm alongside the head. The soldier puts his hand around the back of his head, cupping the back of his own skull, and tucks his head in. Coupled with a move towards the opponent this can cause an attack to skid off the arm and spend its force around the back of the soldier's head – unpleasant but better than taking a blow on the temple. The usual next move is to wrap or 'snake' the attacker's arm to immobilize it, gripping him for a counterattack.

Covering the ribs is just as simple. The soldier drops his elbow and tucks his arm in tight against his ribs, cushioning the ribcage against a blow. Again, this works best with movement to weaken the blow. Cover defences are not ideal – the soldier is still going to get hit, possibly quite hard. They do offer a chance to mitigate the attack and stay in the fight, but covering up is not the option anyone would choose.

Smother Defence

If the soldier can read his opponent's intentions early enough, he can 'smother' the attack, preventing it landing at all. This works well against swinging blows. The soldier lunges forwards and 'jams' the attack. Against a hook punch or swinging attack, he will drive one arm into the crook of the opponent's arm and the other into his shoulder as close to his own elbows as possible. This ensures that his arms do not fold under the impact, and instead transmits all the force of the soldier's forward movement (and that of the opponent) into the attacker.

The intent is not merely to stop the attack. Ideally the opponent will suffer shock and pain and be rocked back on his heels. This allows the soldier to follow up his defence with a takedown or strikes.

Deflection Defences

A thrusting attack (or a straight punch or kick) can be redirected by pushing it to the side. This should be accompanied by movement to the side to increase the margin by which the attack misses, but the soldier should not move too far. Ideally he wants to end up close to the attacker and 'past' the point of the weapon if one is being used. From here, he can counterattack while the opponent must turn to face him and ready his weapon once again.

Deflection defences are instinctive to some extent, which makes them easy to teach when training time is limited. One advantage to deflecting an attack is that the opponent is often taken off balance and must recover before he can attack again.

Smother Defence

**The Smother is defence and counterattack in one.
The defender moves in and drives his forearms into
the attacker's shoulder and the crook of his arm,
causing intense pain and possibly sending the
attacker staggering backwards.**

Deflection Defences

Attacks that are coming straight in, such as a front kick or a knife thrust, can be deflected to the side with a sweeping motion. Meeting the force of the attack head-on is a bad idea; instead the soldier moves down one arm of the Tactical 'Y' and sweeps the attack to the other side. This combines deflection with an element of evasion.

It is possible to do a great deal of damage to a human being by delivering blows, but only if they land hard and/or in the right place. A tough man can take serious punishment and carry on fighting, and soldiers operating in a combat zone rarely have time to batter their enemies into submission. Strikes therefore need to be clinically effective or else so powerful that precision is not necessary.

Military unarmed combat systems make use of a number of techniques that would be inappropriate (and somewhat horrifying) in a less extreme environment. Under civilian law, once an assailant is unable to continue fighting then hurting him further is not legal. After all, it no longer constitutes self-defence when the opponent cannot attack! In a military context, however, an enemy combatant who can recover and rejoin the battle is a serious liability. It is necessary to ensure that this does not happen, and that can mean crippling or killing a downed opponent.

There is a distinction to be made here; murdering a helpless prisoner is a crime, but finishing off an enemy

....

Most military systems mainly teach hand or elbow strikes aimed at the head and neck, plus a few kicks to the legs and body.

3

Striking tools are the mainstay of military unarmed combat systems. They can put an opponent down fast without the need to become entangled in grappling.

Striking Tools

Dropping Elbow Strike

A downwards elbow strike can be delivered to the head or body of an opponent who is bent over. A good target on the body is just under the shoulder blade. Anywhere on the head will get a result; precision is not really necessary.

soldier who has been temporarily downed to prevent him rejoining the fight is sometimes a necessity of survival. Indeed, downing an opponent then finishing him may be the only way to achieve a decisive result in unarmed combat – it is harder than most people think to disable someone who wishes you serious harm.

It is possible to disable an opponent by winding him, i.e. striking his body hard enough to temporarily interfere with his breathing. He can also be rendered unconscious by shaking his brain within the skull. This is usually accomplished by heavy blows to the head, but a hard fall or impact with a wall will sometimes have the same effect. However, most blows have a lesser effect. They may stagger or stun an opponent, opening him up for a follow-up but it is quite hard to take someone out of a fight with a single clean blow.

The human body is designed to protect the vital organs. Skin is resilient and surprisingly thick. Layers of muscle will absorb many blows, while the brain and vital organs are protected by the skull and ribcage. Bones will of course break if hit hard enough, but it is difficult to do this kind of damage to an opponent who is moving around and fighting back. Thus most unarmed combat systems take the approach that if an opponent is to be finished off then it is best to knock him down and then

kick or stamp on his head or body. A soldier's heavy boots are powerful finishing tools.

Striking with the Hands and Arms

The hands and arms are the most accessible striking tools. They are positioned to reach the opponent's head and body without compromising balance by lifting a foot off the ground. With good body mechanics it is possible to deliver a great deal of force to the target. However, that is a double-edged sword. The body part used to strike with is constructed of the same flesh and bone as the target, and the hand in particular has many small bones that can be broken by hitting a skull, helmet or any other hard object.

It is vital that a soldier does not damage his hands, as this may prevent him carrying out his mission and can result in long-term consequences. Thus while the fist is used as a striking tool, other options are generally preferred for striking hard targets like the head. A good, tight fist is reasonably resistant to damage but is best used to hit 'soft' targets on the body.

For harder targets, an open hand is a better option. Various martial arts use similar strikes but these can be highly stylized. All that is really necessary is to pull the hand back so that the fingers are out of the way; the exact position of the fingers is

Special Forces Tip: Breathe!

Breathe out every time you do something. Every strike, every grab, every time you pull or push the opponent. This not only keeps the air going in and out, which is vital in a fight, but it also makes everything you do more powerful.

irrelevant so long as what hits the target is the base of the palm and the fleshy pad opposite the thumb. This can be awkward from some angles, but it is possible to land hooked and straight palm strikes from most angles.

The usual target for palm strikes is the head, and precision is not particularly necessary. A hard blow anywhere on the head will get a result, though the best striking points are the base of the jaw with hooking strikes and slightly upwards to strike the jaw with a straight shot from the front. Palm strikes to the collarbone area are also sometimes useful, not least because they can be used as a combination of strike and push to send the opponent staggering backwards.

Hammerfists use a clenched fist but the striking area is the pad at the base of the fist. They are used for dropping or hooking (inwards or outwards) strikes to the head or body. There is little danger of damaging the hand when striking in this manner. A hammerfist can also

be performed while holding something, striking with the object. A torch, stick, even a tin of food can be used to augment a hammerfist.

Elbow strikes are extremely powerful and use one of the hardest bones in the body as a contact area. Elbows can be straight or hooked, and are equally effective against head or body. Elbows can be used defensively, for example, striking backwards at an opponent who has grabbed the soldier from the rear, or they can be used as short-range attacking tools.

A few specialized strikes are used. A stiff-fingered strike into the throat can kill if it hits the right spot, as can a blow to the throat with the web of the hand between fingers and thumb. Slightly splayed fingers can be used to attack the eyes. These are all open-hand attacks, and there is one additional benefit to not using fists – stress tends to make people keep their fists closed once they have been formed. Leaving the hands open allows a range of strikes and grabs to be used.

Striking with the Hands

The primary striking tools are closed fists against softer parts of the body, such as the kidney area or solar plexus, and the heel of the palm against harder parts such as the jaw. The edge of the hand and stiff fingers can be used against the throat or side of the neck.

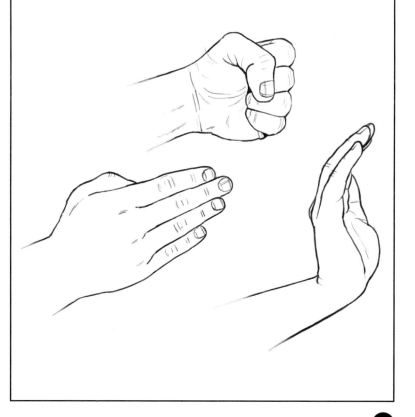

Hammerfist

The Hammerfist is delivered with a hammering action using a tight fist but striking with the fleshy base rather than the knuckles. This protects the hand from damage while still delivering an extremely powerful strike.

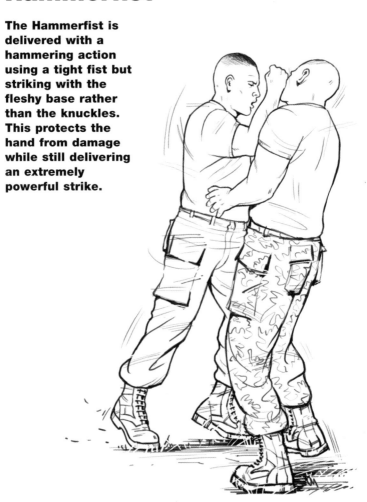

Straight Strikes vs Hooked Strikes

Straight strikes, as the name suggests, travel straight from the soldier to the target. Power is increased by driving forward with the back foot and making sure the shoulder and hip are behind the shot – striking with just the muscles of the arm is ineffective. Straight shots are faster than hooked ones, so it is possible to beat the opponent to the punch. More importantly perhaps, a straight strike occupies the 'centreline' between soldier and target, and effectively defends him from anything coming the other way.

A straight shot may drop the opponent, but even if it does not it should drive him back. This makes it harder for the opponent to fight effectively while the soldier can continue to push forwards with more blows.

Hooking strikes travel along an arc and, as such, have a shorter range than straight shots. They can go around a defensive guard, however, and can land with impressive force. The most instinctive of all blows seems to the wild swing or 'haymaker', but this fairly easy to counter or avoid. It is slow and easy to see coming, though if it lands it will cause real damage.

Trained fighters learn to deliver just as much force with a much tighter and more disciplined hook. This allows the soldier to keep his guard in place for longer in case the opponent attacks and to disguise his intentions so that the strike is more likely to land. Hooking strikes are not delivered just with the arm, but use the mechanics of the whole body, turning the shoulder and hip into the strike and pushing with the back foot. The resulting strike produces a massive impact that can take an enemy out of the fight in one shot.

Commonly, a soldier will launch straight shots as he closes in and then hooked ones as the range decreases or the opponent covers the centreline to defend himself. An opponent whose hands are in front of his face to stop straight shots is open to hooks. If he moves his guard, straight blows once more become an option. However, fights rarely follow such a neat boxing-style progression. More commonly the soldier must simply hit whatever he can see with whichever strike seems most likely to work. It is more important to deliver shock and pain to the opponent with a marginally effective shot than to hesitate whilst looking for that perfect opening.

Eye Strike

An eye strike is usually launched with the lead hand, fingers slightly splayed and curved downwards. It is best to strike slightly upwards, and to hit low rather than high. This allows a poorly-aimed strike to skid into the eyes instead of hitting the opponent's forehead or helmet.

Hooked Punch

A closed fist can be used to strike the head, though there are some risks of hand damage. A hook should be tight, not swung wildly, and will ideally connect close to the tip of the jaw. This jerks the head around and causes 'brain shake', which will disorientate and possibly knock out the opponent.

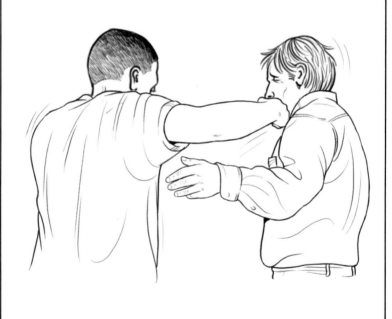

Eye Strike

An eye strike is a fast, light movement and should be done with the lead hand for speed. It will not usually put an opponent totally out of the fight but it will make him flinch and possibly hesitate temporarily. The soldier can put this time to good use. In this case, the eye strike has briefly taken two opponents out of the fight, buying time to deal with the third.

An eye strike is fast and effective, but it is not a fight-ender in its own right. It will make most opponents flinch and allow a follow-up. Anyone stuck in the eyes will turn their head or at least move it sharply, so a palm strike is a better follow-up option than a punch. It is hard to predict exactly where on the head a follow-up shot will land, but a palm shot that arrives anywhere (even on a forehead protected by a helmet) will shake the opponent's brain inside his skull and produce unconsciousness or disorientation.

Chin Jab

A favourite of World War II commandos, the chin jab is one of the few strikes that is effective against a helmeted opponent. It is launched with the strong (rear) hand and ideally comes up into the chin to snap the opponent's head back. The striking area is the base of the palm, and it may be possible to keep the hand in contact with the opponent's head, pushing up and back as the soldier lunges forwards. This exploits the impact to tip the opponent over backwards or at the very least take him off balance.

A missed palm shot that hits cheekbones, nose or forehead will still do some damage and may even knock the opponent out, and it will not endanger the striking hand. It has been claimed that a palm strike up into to the nose can cause death but

Chin Jab

The chin jab is a rising strike under the tip of the chin, which not only transmits force to the brain but also tips the opponent's head violently back and disrupts his posture. It can be followed through with an aggressive forward movement, turning into an opportunistic takedown against a somewhat dazed opponent.

There is a persistent myth that this strike can be delivered to the nose as a killing blow, but that simply does not work. It is, however, tremendously painful, so even a shot that misses the jaw and thus does not cause a knockout will still gain the soldier some advantage.

there is no real evidence that this is possible unless the blow is hard enough to fracture the skull.

Lead/Cross

It takes significant training to become effective at striking with the lead

Lead Hand Punch

A lead hand shot can be thrown with a fist or an open palm. This is not a light, fast 'jab', as in boxing, but a heavy shot with movement and body weight behind it. The soldier wants to get maximum effect from each blow, so he hits hard or not at all. A lead hand shot comes from the guard position with no retraction or 'wind up' and it is not hooked in any way. It goes straight down the middle and interrupts the opponent's intentions, paving the way for an even heavier blow with the strong hand.

Cross Punch

A cross is a straight punch from the rear hand, again thrown with no hooking or retraction. It can be delivered singly or against an opponent who has been grabbed with the lead hand and pulled onto the shot. Most commonly it is thrown as part of a lead/cross combination, coming out as the lead hand is retracted to protect the head. It is possible to strike with the knuckles or to use a palm strike.

Eye Jab/Palm Strike

A variation on the lead/cross combination is to use a fast eye jab to interrupt the opponent's intentions and hopefully make him flinch. This is followed with a palm strike to the chin or whatever part of the head is available.

The opponent may turn his head when the eye jab lands,
so a punch with the knuckles is inadvisable – contact with
the skull could break the soldier's hand. The palm strike
can be delivered as a cross, or the soldier can step in and
turn his strike into a takedown by driving the opponent's
head up and back.

(weak) hand, and some systems do not bother with it at all. However, the lead hand is close to the target and can get there fast, so lead-hand strikes are a useful tool for those with the skill. Palm strikes are preferable, but a punch can also be used.

The lead hand comes straight out from the guard or ready position, going to the target by the shortest route. It is not retracted first – 'winding up' for a shot in such a way slows it down too much and reduces effectiveness. The strike is delivered 'fast and light' all the way to the target, then is driven home by pushing it with the shoulder and hip. The lead arm is retracted quickly to its defensive position, and travels 'fast and light' again. The soldier's body is only tense during the delivery of the strike, and remains relaxed the rest of the time.

A cross is a more powerful blow, again ideally delivered with the palm. It can be launched on its own, or it can follow a lead shot. The soldier might also grab the target with the lead hand and pull him onto the strike. As with the lead strike, the blow travels light until it reaches the target, when it is slammed home and then retracted to guard. It may be possible to grab the opponent and deliver repeated short crosses; with good training these can be almost as powerful as big, long shots.

The cross comes not from the arm but from the back foot, driving forwards with the soldier's entire body weight behind it. It may send the opponent reeling. However, the intent is not to push him but to try to shatter his body with the force of the blow.

Throat and Neck Strikes

The throat is a favoured target in military systems, not least because it is one of the few targets that can be effectively struck on an opponent in combat gear. A hard, precise strike can kill but even a less effective blow will usually cause the opponent to cough and perhaps struggle to breathe. Being struck in the throat also has a profound psychological effect and can put an otherwise effective opponent on the defensive.

A 'web hand' strike using the area between the fingers and thumb can be delivered against the front of the throat. The strike is made with a vigorous forwards thrusting motion, crushing the windpipe and larynx.

A stiff-fingered strike (called a spear hand in some combat systems) is normally directed against the cavity to the side of the larynx. Ideally it is driven in deep and hard as the opponent is pulled onto the blow using the other hand.

The edge of the hand can also be used to strike with, a technique sometimes misnamed a 'judo chop' or 'karate chop'. The target is normally the side of the neck, slipping in through the gap between shoulder and helmet. The throat and

Throat and Neck Strikes

From the front, an excellent throat attack is a 'web hand' strike, using the area between the thumb and fingers as a striking point. This can kill, and will almost certainly cause the opponent difficulty breathing temporarily. From the side, a stiff-fingered 'spear hand' strike can be driven into the carotid sinus (the soft space between the larynx and the muscles that protect the carotid arteries) with similar results.

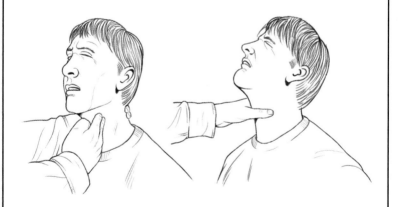

Edge of Hand Strike

The edge of the hand can be used to strike the carotid area (illustrated), which can cause unconsciousness. This strike can slip between the shoulder and the rim of a helmet. There are few other areas that can be effectively attacked with this strike, but the medulla oblongata, situated at the base of the skull, is also a good target if the opponent is suitably positioned.

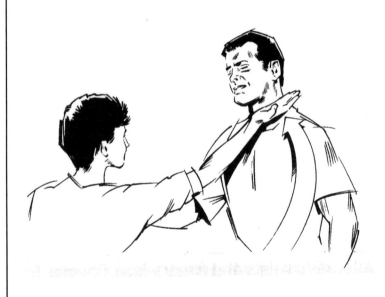

bridge of the nose are also good targets. For this strike the hand is formed as for a spear hand, but the contact area is the side of the hand between wrist and the base of the fingers, on the side opposite the thumb. It is important to keep the fingers together and not let them flick out as this can result in damage.

Body Shots

The fist is an effective striking weapon against softer targets, which makes it useful against the body. However, a blow of this sort is more or less useless against an opponent wearing heavy clothing or body armour, and there is always a risk of striking a hard piece of equipment. That said, not all opponents are fully equipped so the body blow can be useful.

A body shot can be delivered straight or hooked. The straight shot is delivered with a shovelling action coming in under the ribs to attack the diaphragm and solar plexus or the kidney region if the attack is made from the side. The blow should be travelling slightly upwards if possible, and is driven in by pushing the hip and shoulder forwards. The target can be grabbed with the other hand and pulled onto the strike for extra effect.

A hooked body shot uses rotation to deliver power. The arm follows a short horizontal arc – striking upwards or downwards weakens the blow – and is driven home using body rotation, pushing the hip and

shoulder into the blow. A hook to the head is executed in much the same way, but is not a staple of military systems due to the risks inherent in punching a (possibly helmeted) head with a closed fist.

Neither type of body shot is certain to end a fight, but it will severely impair the opponent's capabilities and allow a decisive finish to be achieved.

Cupped-Hand Strike

This strike uses similar mechanics to a hook punch but an open hand is used to hit with. The striking point is not the fingers – that would risk breaking them – but the fleshy base of the palm. Ideally the target is the base of the jaw under the ear, well below the line of an enemy's helmet. This also allows the soldier's fingers to go around the curve of the opponent's head, which further protects them from damage.

However, a hard enough blow anywhere on the head can cause unconsciousness. A shot to the cheekbone or temple can put most opponents down or at least stun them for a follow-up. Whereas striking the head with a fist risks damage to the hand if the contact point is slightly off, a palm strike is much less likely to cause damage to the soldier's hands.

A soldier whose strike is not quite properly placed, and who walks away from his unconscious opponent with

Body Shots

A frontal body shot under the ribs to the solar plexus can take an opponent out of the fight. It can be delivered with the hand palm up, with a shovelling action, or as a piston punch with the fist vertical (illustrated). A slightly upwards blow is far more effective than one travelling downwards.

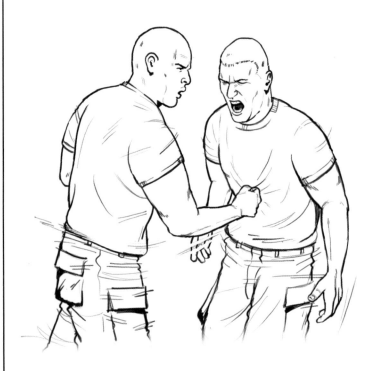

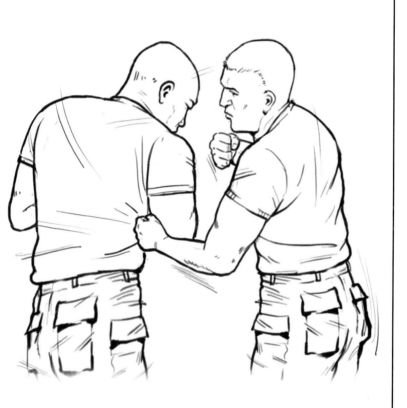

A hooking punch into the kidney area (illustrated above) is also potentially debilitating and can be used to get around an opponent's guard.

Cupped-Hand Strike

The cupped-hand strike follows a similar path to the hook but is more extended. The aim point is just below the ear, striking with the fleshy 'L' at the base of the palm, opposite the thumb. The aim is to deliver maximum blunt force trauma to the opponent's head. The hand will not be damaged whatever part of the opponent's head is struck, so great precision is not a requirement.

nothing more than a sore palm, has won a solid victory. One who smashes his fist on an opponent's skull may be incapable of using his rifle and thus in severe danger.

The hooking cupped-hand strike is not the same thing as 'boxing the opponent's ears'. This is a valid tactic; using a more deeply cupped hand to strike directly over the ear and burst the eardrum using air pressure.

However, the cupped-hand strike is more generally useful as it will get an effect even if it does not land in exactly the right place.

An inside-wrist strike is very similar to the cupped hand strike but, instead of hitting with the hand, the bony area on the thumb side of the wrist is used to make contact. The usual target is the side of the head

and is often followed up by looping the arm around the opponent's head for a headlock.

Elbow Strikes
Elbow strikes are close-quarters striking tools, but this is rarely a problem in hand-to-hand combat.

Defensive Elbow Strike

A backwards thrusting elbow strike will not end a fight but can be used to secure release from an opponent's grasp. This allows the intended victim to turn around and press the advantage gained by the strike.

Offensive Elbow Strikes

The elbow can be used to strike in any close-quarters situation. The primary target is the head, though it is possible to get a good result against the body. Most elbow strikes use a hooking movement; up, down or inwards, but a straight thrusting elbow can be delivered to the back or sides.

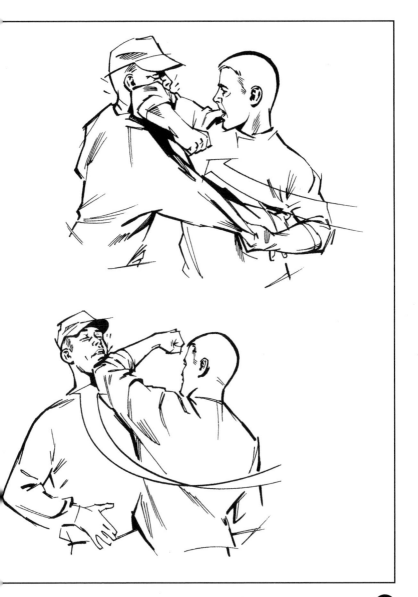

Distance tends to close rapidly, even if that was not the intention of the combatants. It is far more difficult to keep the range open than to close it.

A backwards elbow strike is normally used defensively, against an opponent who is trying for a grab or choke. It is executed by reaching out a little, forwards with the palm up, then slamming the elbow directly backwards. It may be necessary to move a little to the side to line up a strike, and in any case it is imperative to turn to face the opponent as soon as possible.

A dropping elbow is executed in much the same way, but the arm is taken upwards rather than forwards, then the strike is driven down hard. This can be used against an opponent who is bent over, perhaps as a result of a groin strike, or at any time when the soldier is above his opponent, such as when fighting on the ground. It is also possible to drop an elbow into the collarbone when fighting upright at close quarters.

Thrusting elbows come out to the side, though obviously they can be aimed by turning side-on to the opponent. A thrusting elbow is executed by drawing the hand across the body with the arm bent, then driving the elbow hard at the target. Ideally, the soldier will step into the strike and add the weight of his body to the impact. The bony point of an elbow is an excellent striking tool, and this is one of the few strikes that

will have any effect on large muscle groups such as the pectorals.

A forward elbow is launched by pushing the arm forward with the hand up, as if the soldier was reaching up to scratch his ear. As with most other strikes, force is added by pushing shoulder and hip forwards. This is a very close-quarters strike and is mainly used to make space for something bigger. If the elbow is swung upwards instead of forwards then an impact under the opponent's chin can result in a knockout.

Hooking elbows move inward in an arc and are effective against the head or body. For best results, the soldier turns his hand so that the back of his hand is facing him, thumb pointing down. The strike is rotated into the target.

Hooking elbows are often used on an opponent who has been grabbed. One good option is to grab the opponent around the back of the head with one hand and to slam the other elbow into his head. This can be done repeatedly, or the soldier might then grab the opponent's head with both hands and deliver knee strikes.

Striking with the Legs

The legs are very powerful, but there are drawbacks to striking with them. Lifting a foot off the ground compromises a soldier's balance, especially if he is carrying heavy kit. However, kicks are sometimes the only effective way to attack someone

Groin Kick

Military combat systems usually include groin kicks, which are delivered with the toes of the boot. There is no need to worry about damage to a foot protected by boots, and the impact is sufficiently powerful that a kick that hits the thigh or abdomen instead of the groin will still damage the opponent.

in body armour or whose equipment may get in the way of other strikes. Sufficiently heavy impact will cause damage through most protection and, in any case, the legs, a common target for kicks, are rarely armoured.

No military combat system cares much about high kicks. Most kicks are directed to the legs or body, or whatever parts of a downed opponent are available. Many martial arts are performed barefoot, and spend considerable amounts of time training their practitioners how to correctly form the foot to avoid damage. So long as he remembered to put his boots on, a soldier does not need to worry about details like curling his toes back to protect them. Boots are one of a soldier's best weapons in close combat; any opponent who can be knocked down can easily be finished off.

Stab Kicks

A 'stab' kick uses the toe of the boot and can be delivered to any low target. The groin is the ideal choice, and is attacked with an upward swinging motion. The instep can also be used, but the toe does more damage. Other targets include the shin or knee, or the ankles. A heavy boot can break an ankle, but even if it does not the kick will cause intense pain and make it difficult for the opponent to stand on that leg.

Stab kicks can be used 'free', i.e. when the soldier is not in physical

Shin Kicks

A sweeping kick with the side of the boot to the shin is extremely painful and may cause the opponent to lose his balance. This can be used to set up a takedown, using the momentum of the kick and the opponent's natural flinch away from the pain to get his foot out from under him. With his balance thus compromised, he will be much easier to take down.

contact with the opponent, or can be delivered to his lower leg after grabbing him. In this case, they are often used as part of a takedown; kicking away a leg and pulling the opponent over. A sweeping kick with the side of the boot also works well in this manner.

Front Kick

The front kick is a thrusting kick launched directly forwards. It is usually delivered with the rear foot, gaining a lot of momentum along the way. The kick is not swung; the knee is lifted and then the leg is driven out forwards. The ball of the foot is normally used to strike with but boots make this less critical; the soldier may not even notice if his toes make contact with an enemy combatant's body instead of the ball of his foot.

A front kick is normally delivered to the groin or lower body and will fold the target in the middle and/or drive him backwards. The same kick is also used to smash through doors and other obstructions. It is important to push the hips down and forwards as the kick lands to deliver maximum force, especially when breaking open a door that may have hostiles on the other side.

Roundhouse Kick

The roundhouse kick is extremely powerful, though it takes some skill to deliver properly. It is normally launched off the rear leg for maximum

Side Kick

Not all military systems use side kicks as they require considerable skill and a fair amount of space to use. They are very powerful, however, and can send an opponent flying. The soldier lifts his leg and pushes it straight out as if stamping with his heel. If the kick is hooked in any way it will be weak and ineffective. For maximum effect the soldier sets up the kick by stepping towards the opponent, adding his whole body weight to the blow.

Roundhouse Kick

A roundhouse kick is
delivered by lifting
the leg and then
straightening it rather
than trying to swing it up
and round at the same
time. It normally comes
from the rear leg and
incorporates a twisting
action of the body. The
contact point is the
lower shin and instep,
adding the weight of
the boot into the blow.
The soldier does not
flick the kick out then
retract it; instead he
throws it hard and uses
the opponent's body to
stop his kick. The leg
can also be attacked
in this way, in which
case the kick should
be travelling slightly
downwards when
it lands.

Kicking from the Ground

Any downed soldier needs to get up as fast as he can, but it may be necessary to deal with an opponent first. Trying to stand while blows are raining down is unlikely to work.

Instead the soldier gets his feet towards the opponent and kicks out, aiming at the knees or groin. A thrusting kick anywhere on the leg will push the opponent away or perhaps make him fall, creating an opportunity to get up and get back into the fight.

impact. The soldier must turn his lead foot to point in the direction of the kick then begin to rotate in that direction as he brings his kicking leg up. The hip is 'rolled over' so that the knee points at the desired striking point. The leg is then straightened, which accelerates it down an arc to impact the target. The instep and lower shin are used to strike with.

Some martial arts deliver this kick as a sort of flick, pulling the leg back off the target and returning it neatly to the ground. Military systems deliver more force by allowing the target's body to stop the kick, dropping the foot back to the ground at the end of the kick. This brings the soldier very close to the target from where he can use elbow or knee strikes to end the matter. The roundhouse kick is often delivered against the body, but can also be used against the legs. In this case it should be travelling slightly downwards when it lands, buckling the legs and ideally driving the opponent to the ground.

Alternatively, at close range a roundhouse knee strike can be put to use. The mechanics are the same as for the kick but the leg is not straightened; instead the knee is driven along an arc and into the target.

Stomp and Thrust Kicks

The most basic attack with the legs is to stomp on an opponent. This is simply a matter of straightening the leg to drive the heel into the target, and is best done against a downed opponent. Targets include the head and body, but wrists and ankles can also be stomped on to disable the target. A stomp can also be used

Knee Strikes

Knee strikes can be delivered from almost anywhere. A solid hit to the body can be a fight-ender, but a strike to the leg is still effective. An opponent whose leg is damaged cannot move or fight effectively, and can be finished off quickly with additional blows or a takedown.

to attack the opponent's foot while standing.

The same stomping action is the basis for what many martial arts refer to as side kicks or thrust kicks. These come out to the side, as the name suggests, and can be used horizontally to the body or downwards to the legs. The latter is more generally useful.

Attacking the legs is best done from the side, though a stomp to the knee from the front can break a leg quite easily. To execute a stomp kick

the soldier raises his knee and drives his foot sharply into the target, dropping his body weight into the kick and pushing through the target to ensure maximum damage. The leg should be straight and, as with the roundhouse kick, there is no retraction. The aim should be to put the kicking foot back on the ground by pushing it through the target, not to pull it back.

Side Kicks

Side kicks are used by some military systems and can be effective, but they require significant room to execute. The soldier steps towards the target and turns side-on. He lifts whichever leg is nearest the target and brings his knee up high before driving his foot towards the target, heel first. The must be no horizontal or vertical arc to a side kick – it is a

Special Forces Tip: It Doesn't Matter How You Win!

Sport fighters care about rules. Soldiers care about survival. There are no penalties for fighting dirty; indeed there are benefits, like staying alive.

stomp executed out to the side, and any curving motion will weaken it. Stomp-type kicks can be used defensively when on the ground. A soldier who is on his back can kick out at anyone who tries to approach him, aiming to break knees. If he is on the side he will execute a side kick with his higher leg, again with the intent of damaging an assailant's legs and bringing him down.

Knee Strikes

Knee strikes are excellent close-quarters combat tools that require very little skill. They can be delivered 'free' but are best used against an opponent who has been grabbed. The target is normally the groin, lower body or legs but a bent-over opponent can be kneed in the head to finish him off.

A short, sharp knee strike to the thigh is often used as part of arrest & restraint technique when trying to handcuff or control a struggling suspect. The sudden pain and loss of balance acts as a distraction and allows the soldier or police officer to get control of the arms, perhaps applying a restraint hold or handcuffs. The same principle can be used in close-quarters 'vertical grappling', using knee strikes to wear down an opponent or disable his legs.

Roundhouse knees have already been discussed. The simpler straight knee strike is one of the

Ear Bite

Sometimes everything goes wrong. An attempt to strike becomes a wrestling match and the soldier needs to disengage himself. 'Dirty tricks', like biting the opponent, can enable the soldier to gain space for a powerful blow or to escape from a bad situation. The soldier must also be aware that his opponent will not fight fair. One good way to avoid being bitten is not to get involved in grappling.

most instinctive actions of which humans are capable. It is a matter of raising the knee by bending the leg; nothing more. Of course, it must be done violently and some knee strikes are more 'forwards', while others are more 'upwards', depending on the target.

Knees are perhaps most effective from a clinch position. A two-handed head clinch is ideal for delivering this sort of strike. The soldier grabs his opponent around the head with both hands, pulling him forwards and down onto a rising knee to the body or face. Knees can also be delivered in other positions, e.g. while fighting on the ground.

Headbutt

Headbutts are most commonly used in close combat where the soldier can either pull his opponent onto the strike or is held so that he cannot move freely.

It is unwise to headbutt anyone who is wearing a helmet or equipment that can cause injury, but occasionally the tactic is viable.

A headbutt is executed by dropping weight forwards and using the corner of the head, diagonally above the eyebrow, to strike with. A simple rule is that any headbutt that hits the opponent below the eye line will do him significant damage.

It is also possible to execute a backwards or upwards headbutt to secure release from a grab or hold.

Headbutt

Headbutting is always something of a risk, but it can be an effective surprise move. Sometimes it is the only viable option. It is important to avoid a straight forehead-to-forehead clash as this harms both fighters about equally. Instead the corner of the head is used to attack with, against a fragile target like the nose or cheekbone. Rather than a whipping motion, it is better to hold the head still relative to the body and use it as the impact component of a strike delivered with whole-body motion.

4

Although grappling is not the first choice for most combatants, a solid grasp of the mechanics is essential to combat effectiveness under highly fluid conditions.

In a life-or-death situation, with multiple opponents a real possibility, it is often a bad idea to become tied up in grappling. However, grappling offers the soldier or police officer a number of options. In a lower-threat environment, a suspect or prisoner can be restrained and captured or ejected from an area. This may be important when troops are guarding an installation. A variety of people might try to get in for reasons other than causing mayhem.

While it seems reasonable to shoot or incapacitate a gunman or a bomb-carrying terrorist, another approach must be taken with protesters, who may be trying to provoke an over-reaction, or with other 'less dangerous' intruders, such as thieves or zealous journalists. The ability to overpower and render helpless an intruder allows a lower level of force to be used when appropriate.

Snatch and Grab
This also applies to police and military personnel trying to arrest a suspect. Key enemy personnel can be taken alive to provide intelligence or face trial for any crimes (e.g. crimes against humanity or terrorist acts) they have

....

Grappling techniques increase a soldier's capabilities, widening the range of options available to him.

Grappling Tools

committed. Troops and riot police sometimes make 'snatch raids' into a rioting crowd to arrest ringleaders. This is a hazardous operation that may require a rapid switch from detaining a suspect and removing him from the support of the mob, to dealing with a serious attempt to harm or kill the arresting personnel.

Grappling skills are important for other reasons, too. They teach the soldier to deal with being grabbed, something that happens all the time in close-quarters combat. The world's best striking skills are wasted if the soldier is rendered helpless whenever someone manages to catch hold of him. Grappling skills allow the soldier to escape from a grappling situation, and they can also be used to augment striking skills.

A skilled combatant can use his grappling skills in conjunction with striking, or to cause damage to the opponent. It is often hard to deliver a telling blow to an opponent who is moving around, but a skilled grappler can put his enemy where a strike will do the most damage. Alternatively, he may be able to use his skills to break limbs, disarm an enemy or get him on the ground where he is temporarily out of the fight – and can be finished with the boots if necessary.

Head Clinch

If an opponent's head is controlled then there is a limit to how much his body can do, especially if he is being dragged about. The head clinch is commonly used to deliver knee strikes to the body or head. The latter can be difficult; it is hard to pull the head down far enough if the opponent is resisting. Body blows are much more accessible.

Both hands are normally used for a clinch, but a one-handed head clinch does work. The principle in both cases is the same. The soldier cups one hand around the back of the opponent's neck, keeping his elbow down to prevent the opponent from simply ducking out backwards.

A one-handed clinch (also known as a one-handed collar tie) must be accompanied by blows or the opponent will escape quickly.

For a more solid clinch, the soldier places his other hand over the first and pulls the opponent's head down onto his shoulder, breaking his posture and making resistance difficult. Again, the elbows are kept down to prevent escape.

Two-handed Head Clinch

The two-handed head clinch (often referred to as a Muay Thai clinch as it is used extensively in that martial art) is often applied to drag the opponent about, keeping him off balance and disorientated as knee strikes are driven into this body.

Even just one good blow will often make an opponent to double up and weaken, so he can be taken down.

Head Clinch Takedown

Where the head goes, the body follows. Dragging an opponent down by the head is entirely effective. For maximum effect the soldier will slam a couple of knee strikes into the body then throw the opponent face-first into the ground.

There are two good takedowns from this position. The first is aptly called a 'faceplant'. The soldier steps back, dragging his opponent forwards and down. As he falls, the soldier helps him on his way by throwing his head down, aiming at a spot roughly where the soldier's feet were before he stepped back. The opponent will hit the ground hard and face-first.

In the second takedown the soldier takes a step back (with either foot) and drags the opponent forwards and down. He then rotates around whichever foot has not moved using his body weight rather than just the strength of his arms to drag to

Headlocks

Headlocks often happen more or less by accident, as one combatant grabs the other by the head to try to get him under control. From this position it may be possible to bring up a knee into the head or to free one arm for a series of strikes, which the opponent will find it difficult to counter.

opponent around him. As the opponent falls, the soldier lets go and flings him to the ground. He will land on his back at the soldier's feet where he is an easy target for a follow-up.

Coming Out of a Clinch

Normally a soldier who has obtained a clinch will finish from there or transition to a takedown. However, sometimes it is more useful to come back out of the clinch. Trying to pull away is counterproductive and likely to result in being hit, so the slider instead will 'explode' out of the clinch with a barrage of strikes.

When he is ready to come out, the soldier pushes his opponent sharply

backwards with both hands, driving into the crease of the shoulders. He throws his weight into this effort by pushing himself forwards with his rear foot. The opponent will stagger back if this is executed properly, and may spread his hands for balance. This opens him up for a strike. The soldier steps forwards and delivers a powerful palm blow to the head, following up with other strikes. If the opponent goes too far out of reach, a front kick is a good alternative. This is useful, especially if it entangles him with a comrade or sends him crashing into an obstruction.

Arm Wrap/Arm Clinch

The arm wrap or arm clinch is used to immobilize the opponent's striking arm and any weapon he may be holding. It is normally used after a defensive action, such as covering or smothering a hooking blow. As soon as the opponent hits the soldier's defending arm, he 'snakes' it around and locks the opponent's arm tightly to his body. Ideally his forearm is behind the opponent's elbow, which prevents the arm from being pulled straight back.

An arm clinch can also be used offensively; in this case the soldier lunges forwards and secures the opponent's strong arm (usually the right) before he can do anything. However the clinch occurs, the soldier has various options using his other arm. He can grab the opponent

around the head in a one-handed collar tie (see above) and pull his head down whilst retaining control of the arm. This is a good position from which to deliver knee strikes. Alternatively, the soldier can deliver strikes with his free hand. The web-hand strike to the throat is very accessible from here.

Takedown Option

If a takedown is desired, there are three good options. The most accessible is the outer reaping takedown (also know as a rear trip). This is used when the soldier's defence has taken him slightly off to the side. Both of his hands are on the same side of the opponent's head in this case. Snaking the opponent's striking arm with his outer arm, the soldier forces the opponent's head back. This can be done by grabbing his trapezius area and lifting the forearm under the chin, or by putting a hand on his face and shoving up and back.

As the opponent's head is pushed back, the soldier steps in deep and sweeps away his opponent's foot. This will be the foot on the same side as the opponent's striking arm. The combination of head going back and foot going forwards will topple the opponent to the ground. The soldier can yank up on the arm he has trapped in the hope of breaking it, and is well positioned to finish

Arm Clinch

Not all clinches use the head. Immobilizing an arm and keeping the opponent close can be useful as a means to get him under control before attempting a takedown or 'trading up' for a better grip.

Two-Point Takedown

Most takedowns use the same principle of using two points. Here the opponent's upper body is forced back and his leg is taken away forwards. He might be able to deal with either alone, but done together they will result in a heavy fall.

off an opponent stunned by a heavy fall and a possibly broken arm.

The inner reap is performed much the same way, but from a more central position, i.e. the soldier's hands are on opposite sides of the opponent's head. The arm is immobilized in the same manner, and the head is pushed back in much the same way. The soldier puts his leg between the opponent's legs rather than round the outside and hooks away the foot nearest to him. This produces a hard fall but there is a danger of being dragged down with the opponent. If that happens, the best option is for the soldier to try to land knee-first on the opponent's testicles.

As an alternative to the outer reap, the soldier can 'pass' the opponent's arm by slapping it sharply upwards and ducking quickly past. He will come up behind the opponent's arm, from where he can reach around his neck to place the bony inside of his wrist alongside the opponent's carotid arteries. His outer hand grabs his own hand or wrist and pulls in tight, keeping his head against the opponent's shoulder for protection.

This applies a strangle that can be used to render an opponent unconscious or even kill him, and is extremely painful as well. The intensity of the hold can be varied in order to keep someone under control without harming him, and the strangle put back on hard at need.

Alternatively, the opponent can be dumped hard onto the ground by using a rotational movement similar to the one used from a head clinch. This time the outer foot must move back, so if the soldier's right arm is around the opponent's neck applying the strangle, he must rotate anti-clockwise.

As the soldier rotates, he pulls the opponent round and down with arms and body weight, letting go as he starts to fall. Impetus can be added by throwing the opponent into the ground where he will land on his back or side and be easy to finish off. If the soldier keeps hold, he will follow the opponent down and land in a dominant position with a strangle ready to be applied. However, this option is not ideal for the battlefield; it is better to dump the opponent to the ground and stand over him raining down blows than to become entangled with him.

Joint Locks and Destructions

Most of what are called 'locks' or 'submissions' in martial arts are actually techniques intended to destroy joints by taking them past their normal range of motion. Used with careful control these techniques can be used to restrain an opponent or, in sporting competition, make them 'tap out' or concede the bout. The pain these techniques cause and the threat of damage to the joint

Outer Reaping Takedown

The outer reap (or rear trip) can be performed from many entries. Here, the soldier moves forwards from a mutual grab situation, taking his opponent off balance by pushing his head and upper body backwards (A). He then takes one foot away from under the opponent by 'reaping' it away with his foot (B). Driving the upper body down makes the opponent fall harder (C).

A

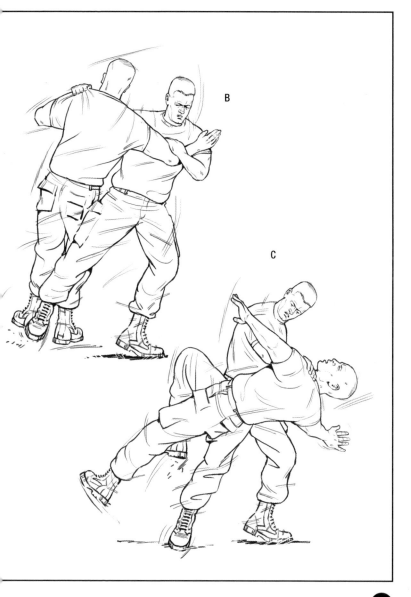

B

C

Standing Strangle/ Outer Wheel Takedown

The soldier digs the inside of his wrist into the opponent's neck and pulls him in tight, applying a painful strangle. The opponent can be 'choked out' from here or can be dumped to the ground by a sharp rotating action.

enables the user to control an opponent. This can be used for arrest or restraint, or to secure a prisoner.

However, in open combat the main uses for joint locks are to put someone in a vulnerable position or to break a limb. In the latter context, locks are applied hard and fast, and with the full intent of destroying a joint. This has the advantage of allowing the soldier to move on to his next opponent without becoming entangled.

Thus the same body of technique can be used for a variety of purposes by police and military personnel; the only difference between the two situations is the intent and the level of force applied. Someone who struggles against a restraining joint lock can damage their own joints, putting themself out of the fight even as they try to escape.

Wrist Locks

Wrist locks are primarily used to disarm an opponent or to control someone for arrest. They are far less effective in a straight fight than many martial artists prefer to believe. It is virtually impossible to catch a wrist in the middle of a fight, which makes many potential applications invalid. It is no coincidence that the creator of Krav Maga called wrist locks 'cavaliers', by which he meant fanciful and flashy techniques.

Wrist-locking techniques fall into 'if the opportunity presents itself'

category. If the arm can first be controlled then a wrist can usually be gripped well enough to apply a lock, and sometimes the opponent will give the soldier a chance to perform a wrist lock by grabbing him. Occasionally the opportunity just happens in the chaos of a fight, and if so it can be taken for all it is worth. But overall, wrist locks are relatively low-percentage techniques and do not form part of the soldier's front-line repertoire.

Inner Wrist Lock

The 'inner' wrist lock is performed by grabbing the hand and twisting it so that the thumb is pointing down and it will not turn any further. The soldier then tries to force the hand to rotate about a point close to the large bone that sticks out of the wrist, as if trying to feed the opponent's little finger into his nose. Pushing the hand towards the opponent can increase the effect.

Most people react to this lock by dropping into a crouch, trying to reduce the pain. This puts them in a position to be kneed in the face or chest. It is hard to maintain this position, however; the opponent will usually wriggle out of the lock unless it is followed up with another technique. Locking the wrist in this manner can be done from other positions, e.g. when a suspect is face-down on the ground and needs to be secured for handcuffing.

Wrist Locks

The wrist can be locked by twisting the hand round
as if trying to push the palm onto the thumb, or by
rotating it as if trying to push the thumb to where
the little finger currently is. Getting control of a wrist
in the middle of a fight is, however, problematical.

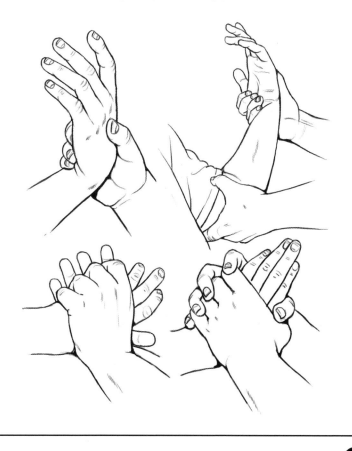

Outer Wrist Lock

The 'outer' wrist lock takes the hand the other way. The soldier grabs the opponent's hand with his thumb on the back of the hand and twists it so that the opponent's thumb is pointing forwards and his fingers upwards. The opponent's wrist must be pushed close to his body or he will escape. This lock can be used violently to snap the forearm or can be applied more slowly to force the opponent down and to the side.

Folded Wrist Lock

The folded wrist lock folds the wrist at 90 degrees and strains its tendons. If it is done violently, these will tear and render the hand useless. The arm must be immobilized to prevent escape. This technique is used in 'come-along' holds but can also be used as a joint break. One way to do this is to fold the wrist by grabbing with fingers and thumb around the base of the opponent's hand and then slamming his elbow into something solid behind him, such as the ground or a wall. This can be used as a finish against a downed opponent, rendering his weapon hand useless.

Arm and Shoulder Locks

Arm locks are far more accessible than wrist locks as the arm is easier to get hold of. There are two broad types; those that attack the shoulder joint and those that damage the elbow.

Both types can be applied from a variety of positions; standing up, on the ground and anywhere between.

Arm Bar

The 'arm bar' is a common submission hold used in competitive martial arts, and can be used as a break or a restraint. If applied as a restraint, it can still be used to break the elbow but this can be difficult. The decision thus needs to be made whether to go straight to a break or to try to control the opponent instead.

One common way to apply an arm bar is against an opponent who sends a straight arm forwards, e.g. with a punch or a grab. The soldier steps to the outside of the arm and secures it by hooking the opponent's arm (over the top or underneath, it does not really matter) with his own. Jamming the opponent's wrist or forearm between biceps and forearm works well, or the forearm can be 'scooped' with a hand curled into a hook. Either way, the arm must be held against the soldier's body and prevented from moving.

To break the arm, the soldier strikes close to the opponent's elbow with a point close to his own, driving through as far as he can whilst pulling the opponent's wrist and forearm towards himself. This creates a shearing action that will tear the elbow joint apart.

Folded Wrist

Another way to damage the wrist is to fold it beyond its range of motion. If the opponent's elbow is slammed into the ground with the wrist folded in this manner, extensive damage will result.

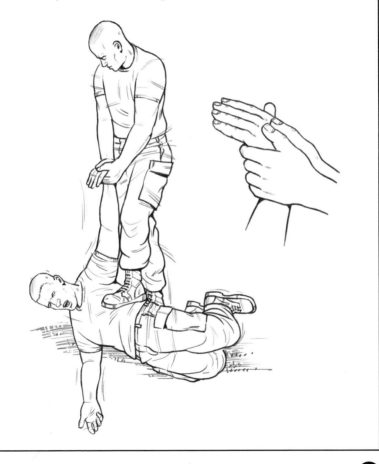

Arm and Shoulder Lock

The opponent's arm is captured by 'snaking' an arm around it. From the inside, the arm goes over the top, down the outside and inward underneath, ending up behind the elbow. The hand then grips the other arm, which is extended to grasp the opponent's shoulder.

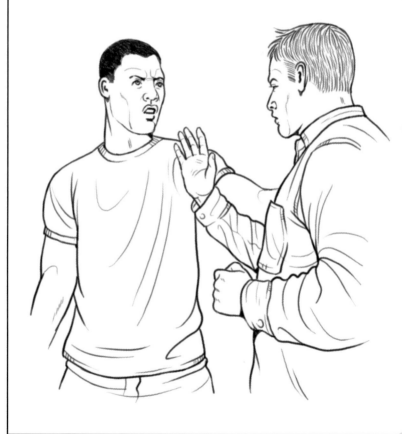

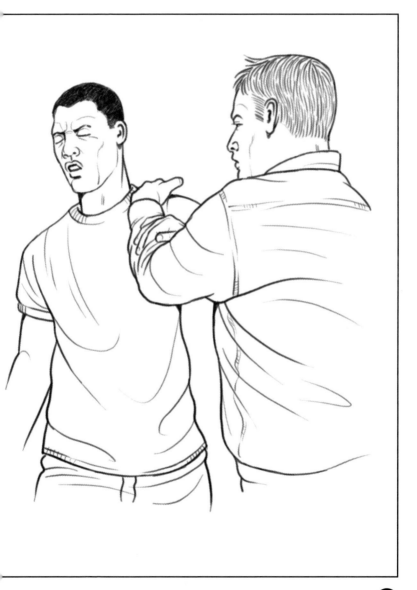

Arm Lock Restraint

With the opponent's arm secured by looping an arm around it, the soldier pushes the opponent down, grinding his forearm across the opponent's triceps. The opponent will end up bent over with his arm locked out to the side.

Restraint and Control

For a restraint or control, the soldier pushes his own arm close to the hand against the back of the opponent's arm and rolls it over by grinding his bony forearm forwards across the opponent's triceps. Again, the hand is pulled towards him and the soldier steps in, as if trying to put his hip in the opponent's armpit. The opponent will bend forwards and down to escape the pain; it is possible to drive his face into the ground with this movement.

To secure a restraint from this position, the soldier puts the elbow of whichever arm is closest on the opponent's back and pushes down hard, moving his hand to the elbow. The opponent is now pushed down by his back and elbow, while his arm is pulled painfully straight by the soldier's other hand.

The commonest shoulder lock is the classic 'arm up the back' or 'hammer lock', normally applied to an opponent who has been controlled in other ways. The subject's arm is bent and pushed as far as possible up his back. This facilitates handcuffing or can be used as a come-along, but can be escaped by moving forwards. Thus the other hand or arm is normally used to control a standing subject by gripping the collar or applying a choke hold. A subject who is face-down on the ground can simply be pushed down.

Another way to obtain this position is to drive a hand through between the opponent's arm and body, then step around 180 degrees so that the soldier is standing beside the opponent facing the same way. As he moves around, the soldier brings his hand up and back towards himself as if he was going to put his hand over his ear. This bends the subject over and locks his shoulder. If his arm bends, the soldier can reach over with his other hand and grab the wrist, pulling it up the subject's back to apply a hammer lock. Care must be taken not to allow the opponent to move forwards and out of this lock. If the arm stays reasonably straight, the shoulder is locked and can be broken by kicking away the subject's supporting foot. His body weight will pull his locked arm out of the shoulder joint.

Chokes and Strangles

The terms 'choke' and 'strangle' are often used interchangeably, and in practice most choking/strangling techniques do a little of both. Correctly speaking, a choke cuts off the body's air supply by constricting the windpipe and a strangle cuts the blood supply to the brain by compressing the carotids.

Being choked is a frightening experience and will cause most opponents to struggle violently. It can be resisted for some time, and can take a while to subdue an opponent

Hammer Lock

The classic 'arm up the back' lock is effective unless the opponent can step forwards out of the lock. The opponent needs to be secured by pushing him down or against something, or held with one hand and locked with the other.

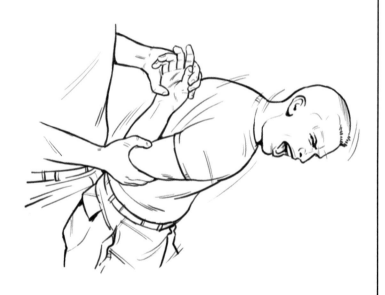

even if it is properly secured. A strangle, on the other hand, can cause unconsciousness in 5–10 seconds and death soon afterwards if properly applied. Some strangles are referred to as 'sleeper holds' as they are most commonly used to render the subject unconscious.

Chokes and strangles can be used as controls, being tightened or loosened as necessary to keep the subject under control.

Even a partially-applied choke can rapidly wear down an opponent as it makes it very difficult to supply the large quantities of oxygen used up by the body in a fight. The first priority for anyone being choked or strangled is to free themselves, which can be exploited by an opponent. A subject who is struggling to pull a choke off his throat is not attacking, for example, and this gives his enemy a head start on his next move.

Rear Naked Choke

The 'Rear Naked Choke' is often used to eliminate sentries or any opponent who has been taken by surprise. One arm is slipped around the subject's throat, with the bony forearm across the windpipe. It is secured by pushing the other arm over the subject's shoulder and placing the hand on the biceps. The soldier then curls his arm back and places his hand

on the back of the subject's head. Pushing the head forwards whilst pulling the arm into the throat applies a choke.

The subject must be prevented from escaping by pulling him back, off balance, so that he falls back against the soldier choking him. If this causes the soldier to fall, he must hold the choke in position and keep squeezing wherever he lands, even if he falls hard.

Variants on this choke include a one-armed hold used to control an opponent, perhaps to use them as a human shield. This leaves the soldier's other hand free. Again, the subject must be bent backwards to prevent escape. His arm can be grabbed with the soldier's other hand and pulled back to prevent him from drawing a weapon or pulling the choke off. This position will not disable an enemy but it will control him.

In order to render the opponent unconsciousness even more efficiently and swiftly, the soldier can reach further around so that his biceps and forearm rest on the subject's carotid arteries on the sides of the neck. Squeezing will cut off the blood supply to the brain and unconsciousness will rapidly follow. Alternatively, it is possible to reach across the opponent's throat and inside his collar, gripping his clothing and pulling it tight across the carotid.

Rear Naked Choke

The rear naked choke is applied by placing an arm across the opponent's throat and locking it in place with the other arm. The choke is not pulled back; the opponent's head is pushed down and forwards. Bending him backwards makes it much harder to resist the choke.

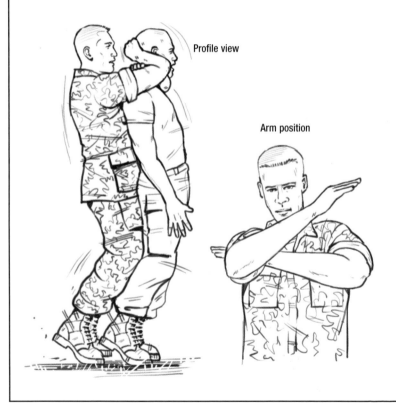

Profile view

Arm position

The opponent must be prevented from pushing his chin down in an attempt to stop the choking arm from being placed across his windpipe. Thus the choke must be put on hard and fast before the opponent can react.

Scissor Choke

Against an opponent who is up against something or on the ground, the scissors choke is applied by gripping tightly inside the collar with the arms crossed and pushing the elbows towards the hands. An effective defence is to push the elbows together, but it must be applied early before the choke is locked in place.

Scissor Choke

This can be done with one hand from the rear; from in front the other hand must also be employed. A 'scissors' choke, with both hands inside the opponent's collar, is accomplished by pulling the subject's head forwards and down. A similar choke can be applied with one hand inside the collar and the other pulling down on the opposite lapel, locking the choke in with the opponent's own clothing.

Bar Choke

A 'bar choke' uses the forearm across the windpipe from the front. This works when the opponent is pushed up against a wall or other obstruction, or when he is on his back on the ground.

To apply this choke against a standing opponent, it is secured by putting the other hand around the back of the opponent's head and placing the hand on the soldier's biceps. He then tries to squeeze his hand and elbow together.

However, this choke leaves the opponent's hands free. If he can reach a knife, the soldier will be killed and even if he cannot, the opponent may be able to fight clear. Thus this choke is mainly used one-handed against an opponent who is jammed against something. It can also be used with less force to hold someone in place.

113

Bar Choke

A simple bar choke, with the forearm across the throat, is effective if the enemy cannot move backwards. It will work best on the ground with body weight to assist, but is also effective against a wall. A useful defence is to push the elbow towards the opponent's hand, causing the choke to slide off.

5

Subjects are often taken down during an arrest or capture procedure, so groundfighting skills are of use to those who wish to take others captive or to resist such an attempt. In open combat, the last thing a soldier wants to do is go to the ground with an opponent, where he may be vulnerable to additional opponents. Sometimes, however, it is unavoidable and so the soldier must be prepared for all eventualities.

The ideal situation has the soldier upright and his opponent down on the ground. From here a stomp or kick with the toe of the boot will usually end the matter. If that situation is reversed, then the soldier's best option is to turn his feet to face the opponent and kick out with either a side or straight kick depending on his body position.

If he is about to be kicked or stomped from the side, the soldier must roll towards the attacker, perhaps stopping the kick with his arms, and grab the opponent around the legs. He can then bring the kicker down or use him as an assist whilst climbing to his feet. The opponent will be able to do little damage to the soldier as he is climbing up him, and

· ·

Groundfighting requires a different set of skills to 'stand-up' combat. Grappling skills can be used to set up strikes or to escape from a difficult situation.

Going to ground is extremely hazardous in all-out combat, but the soldier must be prepared in case it happens. For the police officer, many handcuffing attempts take place on the ground.

Groundfighting Tools

Knee Drop

Rather than joining the opponent on the ground, it is often possible to finish him off with a 'knee drop', i.e., by plunging down to land on the opponent with body weight behind a knee to the head or body.

Law Enforcement Tip: Get Up!

A downed officer is in big trouble, especially if he faces multiple opponents. He must get to his feet as fast as possible where he has the best chance to defend himself.

if he falls then at least the odds are now even, with both combatants on the ground.

For all the impressive submissions seen in sport martial arts, the basic tool in a soldier's ground combat arsenal is 'ground and pound', i.e. getting above the opponent and battering him senseless. However, it is important not to fixate on winning a ground fight to the point where the soldier is then stabbed or shot in the back; a better option is usually to do enough to be able to get up, and to return to an upright position.

'Dirty Tricks'

When fighting an opponent who is willing to kill, with no referee to ensure fair play, it makes sense to employ every dirty trick possible. This gives soldiers a range of options that are not available to people who have to fight fair. Of course, these options are also available to the enemy.

A soldier who is at a disadvantage in a fight on the ground can short-circuit the whole process by pulling a knife or grabbing a rock to bash his

enemy's head in. Even if no weapon is available, he has various ways of evening the odds.

'Fish-hooking' can be used to force an opponent's head in a chosen direction. This means hooking a finger or thumb inside the corner of the mouth (taking care to avoid the teeth) and pulling in the desired direction. Fingers and thumbs can be dug into eye sockets or the soft parts of the throat to obtain what is called 'pain compliance' from the opponent. In other words, he may relinquish an otherwise dominant position to get away from the pain of a finger in his eye.

A soldier involved in a ground fight will use every possible opportunity to hurt his opponent, delivering sneaky knee strikes, headbutts and bites. Elbows can be used to strike with or ground into the opponent's ribs or face. A single knuckle driven into the ribs under the arm causes immense pain. It is also possible to grasp and pull or twist at ears, lips, noses or any piece of flesh that can be grabbed; the opponent's flinch may be enough to allow the soldier to escape or reverse a disadvantageous position.

Dirty Tricks

Sport fighting specifically forbids a number of dirty tricks, but there are no rules in a fight for survival. Attacks to the face and neck require little space or force to be an effective distraction. They can be used standing up or on the ground.
Any part of the face can be grabbed and pulled or twisted, and thumbs or knuckles dug into any soft area will make the opponent flinch, which can be turned to an advantage.

None of these measures will end a fight, but they give the soldier a chance to regain the initiative and begin fighting back. They can also be used, of course, when the soldier is winning. There is no requirement to fight fair at any time, winning or losing.

Positions, Defences and Escapes

The commonest position that anyone fighting on the ground is likely to find themselves in can politely be termed a 'tangle', e.g. half in and half out of a doorway, amid overturned furniture with arms and legs flailing everywhere. It is extremely difficult to achieve anything – escape, arrest or subdual of an enemy combatant – from such a position.

Sport groundfighters have a phrase: 'position before submission', which sums up a tactical necessity. Namely, it is necessary to get a dominant position before attempting anything decisive. A dominant position simply means being above the opponent and situated to at least partially control his options. From here the soldier can look for a finish or an escape; if he is on his back fighting upwards he will be severely disadvantaged.

Thus the first requirement in a ground fight is to get on top of the opponent and achieve a measure of control over him. From here, the soldier can make his next move; to look for a finish or to break off and

escape, perhaps getting up and grabbing a weapon.

The Mount

The most instinctive dominant position is the 'mount'. The soldier is astride his opponent, with his weight pressing down on his chest or abdomen. From here it is easy to rain down blows and relatively simple to break off and escape. It is possible for the fighter on the bottom to strike upwards at the opponent's head and to throw hooking strikes into his body but gravity is not on his side and he is unlikely to win a punching match.

The best chance to escape the mount is as it is being established. Once the opponent has settled into position he can be hard to dislodge, unless he sits right up to drop a heavy blow. If he does this, a new chance to escape is presented. The escape at this point is simple – the soldier brings up one knee and tries to bump the opponent so that he falls forwards. As he does so, the soldier grabs him under the arms or along the ribs and throws him over the soldier's head, then quickly rolls clear and gets to his feet.

If this fails, the first requirement is to prevent the opponent exploiting his position. That means grabbing his arm or head and pulling him down so that he cannot strike. He can then be rolled off the soldier. It is important to hook the leg and arm on the side towards which the opponent is to be

Preventing the Mount

If the opponent cannot be kept away by kicking at him, it may at least be possible to stop him taking the mount. The defender has managed to get one leg in the way, preventing the opponent from establishing his chosen position.

Establishing the Mount

An opponent who sits up high and tries to drop blows down straight away can be dislodged fairly easily. More dangerous is the opponent who keeps his weight low, establishing his mount position, then pops up to start striking when he is ready.

rolled, preventing him putting a hand or foot out to preserve his position.

The soldier pushes down with the opposite foot and rolls his opponent diagonally over, possibly assisting the movement with some pain compliance. This can be a thumb dug into the neck or a single knuckle twisted into the ribs. As an alternative, the soldier might twist the opponent's head in the direction he wants him to go.

Side Control

'Side control' is a strong position to be in. The soldier lies across his opponent, chest to chest, and holds him down with his weight. From here it is easy to slam his elbows or knees into the opponent's body and head.

Escaping side control can be achieved two ways. The simplest is brute force; the soldier drives both arms between himself and the opponent, palms up, and essentially lifts and throws him over his head. He then rolls and scrambles to his feet, ideally getting there quicker than the opponent and delivering a kick while the enemy is vulnerable.

The alternative method is to hold the opponent's head down with one arm whilst forcing the other elbow under his hip. Driving down hard with the foot and lifting with the elbow, the soldier rolls his opponent over and lands on top of him. He follows up with elbow and knee strikes to prevent the opponent from doing the same thing to him.

Knee Ride

'Knee on' or 'knee ride' is a good place to be because it holds the opponent down (and causes him both pain and difficulty in breathing) whilst the soldier is more or less upright and can see what's going on around him easily enough. From here, disengagement is easy, as is delivering heavy blows to the head. A variant of this position can be used when the opponent is partly on his side, such as after he has landed from a reaping takedown. One or both knees can be placed on the ribs or head (or both) as a hold-down or dropped in hard to crack bones. This is called a 'knee drop' and is a highly effective finish to a downed opponent.

The only really effective defence against a knee ride is to push the leg to one side whilst carrying out a motion known as 'shrimping', which means turning partially sideways and bending the middle of the body out of the way. The opponent's knee falls to the ground and the soldier can scramble to his feet. He may use the opponent to assist with this, basically climbing up him to get back to an upright position.

The Guard

The other common groundfighting position is 'guard'. This is not a

Side Control

Side control gives the dominant fighter a great many options. It is hard to dislodge if he keeps his weight well cantered but if he is too far across, he can be rolled off by pushing one arm under his hip and lifting while pushing his head down. Rolling with him places the defender in a dominant position.

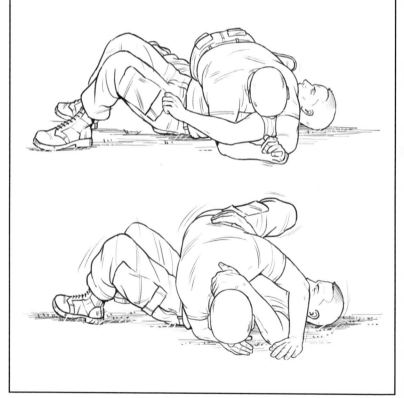

Knee Ride

A 'knee-on' or 'knee-ride' position causes pain and makes it hard to breathe. The only real answer is to push the knee to the side so that it slides off, which can be relatively easy if it is not well centered, and virtually impossible if it is well placed.

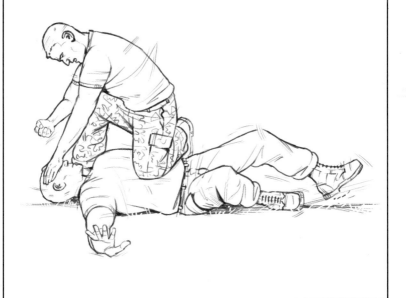

dominant position – the soldier is on his back – but it allows the opponent to be controlled and stops the situation becoming any worse. The soldier grabs his opponent and pulls him down to prevent him dropping blows onto the soldier's face. He locks his ankles together around the opponent's back (this is called a 'closed guard') to prevent him getting up or changing position.

Some sport fighters become highly skilled at fighting from guard and will 'pull guard' by going voluntarily to their back from where they will apply a variety of submissions. This can give the impression that guard is an offensive option but for the soldier it absolutely is not. Guard is a defensive position used to stop things getting any worse. As soon as possible, the soldier must get out of this position and achieve dominance.

Rather than looking to submit his opponent from guard, the soldier needs to get up and back into the fight as quickly as possible. This is accomplished by opening his guard (unlocking the ankles) when he is ready to go and shrimping (as described above) to open up a slight gap on one side. The soldier then places his foot on the opponent's thigh or hip, and kicks the leg away whilst rolling the opponent to that side. Making use of a head twist or pain-compliance technique will assist with this motion.

The Guard

A closed guard (ankles locked together) restrains the opponent from moving into a more advantageous position. Pulling his head down also helps keep him under control until the defender is ready to try to escape.

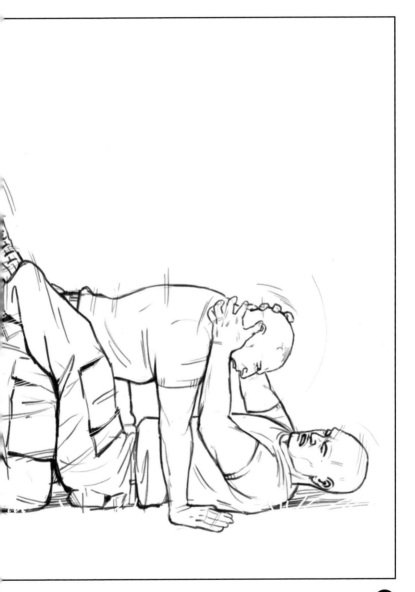

Guard Pass

An open guard (ankles not locked together) can be passed by simply pushing one leg down and climbing over it. The dominant fighter must keep weight on the defender to avoid him rolling clear or, worse, turning the attacker over and getting on top.

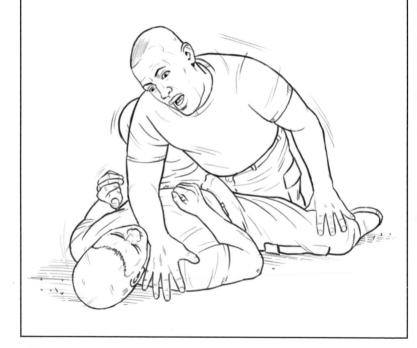

Special Forces Tip:
Hit Him In The Head – A Lot

The shortest and most direct route is often the best. In this case that means delivering repeated blows to an opponent's head until he falls down. It's not clever or pretty, but it gets the job done.

Rolling the opponent over in this manner will place the soldier in a mount position from where he can deliver a rain of elbows and palm strikes, hammerfists and possibly a bar choke to subdue his opponent. This is advisable only when facing a single opponent, however. Under most circumstances the soldier is better off getting to his feet as fast as possible.

Getting Up

The main goal when fighting on the ground should be to get up; the soldier is simply too vulnerable on the ground to stay there for long. However, even from a dominant position it is likely that the opponent will be able to pull the soldier back down. Judicious use of elbows and thumbs driven into fleshy areas or eyes will discourage this; an opponent for whom hanging on is extremely painful will likely let go.

Sometimes it is necessary to hit the opponent or otherwise subdue him in order to facilitate an escape. If so, then it must be done. Simply trying to get up and step away will otherwise result in being grabbed around the ankles and brought down.

If the soldier has found himself in position above the opponent, e.g. standing over him or in a knee-ride position, he can use a 'tactical dismount' to get clear. This means pushing the opponent's head so that his eyes and face point away from the soldier, preventing him being able to see what is happening. The soldier then moves around to the opponent's head and steps away. It is hard to reach in that direction, so this reduces the chance of being grabbed as the soldier moves away. However, in a lethal combat situation the soldier will probably deliver a kick or stomp to the head from this position, making the question of disengaging rather simpler.

131

Making Space, Getting Up

A downed soldier must get up as soon as he can, but simply standing up is often not possible. He must make some space, perhaps by kicking out at the attacker, then get to his feet as quickly as possible.

Sometimes, kicking out causes an attacker to fall on the defender, which is bad but at least better than lying on the ground being stomped or kicked.

PART TWO:
APPLICATIONS

A tool is only as useful as its user lets it be. A weapon is no threat to anyone if it is kept holstered or unloaded, or if the user cannot utilize it. That may happen thanks to incompetence or unwillingness, but the effect is the same.

The same applies to the unarmed combat 'tools' discussed in the previous chapters. They are only as effective as the user allows them to be. It is not enough to know dozens of clever variations on the reaping takedown; what makes it effective is the user's willingness and ability to apply the technique to get a result in combat.

Mind-set is vital. A soldier in combat must be willing to take some risks and do some damage, or he will be unable to make use of his unarmed combat tools. He must also know how and when any given technique will work.

Of these two concepts, offensive spirit is the most important. Doing something slightly sub-optimal right now, and driving through to a hard-fought victory, is much better than waiting for the perfect opportunity to present itself.

An unarmed opponent is still dangerous. Whether he is trying to beat a downed police officer to death, capture a disarmed soldier or is simply fighting with his bare hands for lack of anything better, someone who intends to do harm can usually succeed. It is the mind-set of the opponent that is the most dangerous thing – someone who has a gun or knife but is unwilling to use it is less dangerous than a homicidal maniac who does not have a weapon to hand but is intent on murder.

Additionally, police and military personnel must be aware that an apparently unarmed opponent could have a handgun or knife on his person, or a larger weapon nearby. Police going into a house to make an arrest may face a suspect who has grabbed a kitchen knife, and soldiers may be attacked with sticks or rocks picked up from the ground. This is another reason why combat cannot be allowed to go on for a lengthy period; the longer it takes to subdue the opponent, the more likely it is that he will grab a weapon or someone else will join the fight.

As a rule, personnel will not usually attempt to arrest an armed suspect using unarmed skills. Weapons, or the threat of their use, are the preferred

. . . .

An unarmed opponent is more likely to kick or grapple than one who has a weapon in his hand.

6

Unarmed does not translate to 'not dangerous'. It is the intent of the opponent that matters, not the weapons he has to hand.

The Unarmed Opponent

method. Police have a variety of less-lethal weapons available and might use incapacitant gas or sprays, batons or 'stun guns' in addition to specialist ammunition designed to disable rather than kill a suspect.

Military personnel rarely have access to such a broad spectrum of threat responses. Their weapons are designed to be lethal, creating an all-or-nothing situation. Their training, too, is different. Even a paramilitary police unit, like a SWAT or hostage-rescue team, is first and foremost a civilian law enforcement asset and has an appropriate mind-set. The military response to an 'unarmed' opponent who produces a weapon may be rather more immediately fatal.

However, there are many occasions where both law enforcement and military personnel must deal with an unarmed opponent without using lethal force – or lack a weapon and so have no option. Arrest and restraint methods are taught to soldiers deploying on peacekeeping duties but are always backed up by more robust unarmed combat methods and, of course, firearms.

Pre-Emptive Attacks

The best way to win a fight is to pre-empt the opponent, ensuring that he does not get a chance to do whatever he has in mind. For the civilian acting in self-defence there needs to be some clear indication that the opponent intends to attack, but for police and military personnel a pre-emptive action is often justified by the presence of a hostile combatant or suspect. There is no requirement to wait for the enemy to attack or a suspect to flee before making a move, though any actions taken must be proportionate and reasonable.

Pre-Emptive Choke/Restraint
This is an application of the Rear Naked Strangle. The soldier obviously needs to be behind the

Law Enforcement Tip: Act Decisively!

Police officers will often try to calm a situation down, perhaps persuading the suspect to surrender without a fight. They have to decide whether or not this is likely to work, and if not then when and how best to act. Once the situation has 'gone physical' it cannot be de-escalated. The officer must act decisively at the most opportune moment; he may not get another chance.

Special Forces Tip: In Range

The only reason for being within attack range of an enemy is to attack. If you're not attacking you're open to attack yourself. So either stay out of range or go on the offensive. There is nothing in between; nothing that leads to victory, anyway.

subject to apply the technique, which can be used to kill, subdue or merely control the opponent.

From the front, it is possible to spin the opponent around using a movement called an 'elbow scoop'. The soldier grabs the opponent's nearest arm at the elbow and pulls it across his body in a curve. If the opponent's left hand is nearest then the soldier will use his right hand for this movement.

At the same time he steps diagonally to the side so that he moves to meet the opponent's back, ending up in close chest-to-back contact. The arm that was not used to pull now loops around the throat and drags the head back, taking the subject off balance. The pulling arm is then brought up to complete the Rear Naked Strangle.

From behind, this is a simple matter of sneaking up close and applying the choke. In this context it is used to take out sentries, though often instead of a choke hold the soldier will put his hand over the enemy's mouth to silence him and use a knife to quickly eliminate the sentry.

Pre-Emptive Strike

Against an opponent who is ready and facing the soldier, it is not usually possible to go straight in with a grappling attack. If surprise can be achieved, then a pre-emptive cupped-hand strike or chinjab can be an effective opening move. For example, if the opponent thinks he has control of the situation or does not know the soldier is a hostile combatant, he may be open to a surprise attack while he is talking, ordering the soldier to surrender or asking who he is. This creates an opportunity to take him out of the fight in one shot and escape or deal with any companions he might have. These pre-emptive strikes are executed in exactly the manner shown in the previous chapter.

An opponent who has his hands up and is moving to attack is a different matter. It will be necessary to open him up for the decisive movement. The principle is

Elbow Scoop and Choke/Restraint

The soldier 'scoops' the opponent's arm by grabbing the elbow and pulling across her body and towards her. At the same time she steps out and to whichever side the scoop was performed on, turning so that she is chest-to-back with the opponent. Either arm can then be looped around the opponent's neck, pulling him in tight by the throat. He can be simply held or choked out, depending on the situation.

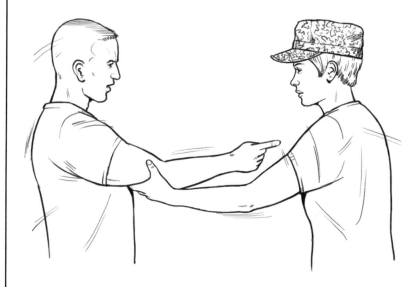

Pre-Emptive Dirty Fighting

The soldier fires a fast lead-hand eye strike (A), causing the opponent to flinch. This creates an opportunity to throw a strong-hand strike to the head. Alternatively, the soldier might just go straight in and grab the opponent around the head, followed by a knee to the groin (B). Ideally the opponent will be defenceless as he will still be mentally and physically out of the fight from the eye strike. As he doubles up, the soldier steps back, grabs him and throws his head downwards, driving him face-first into the ground (C).

A

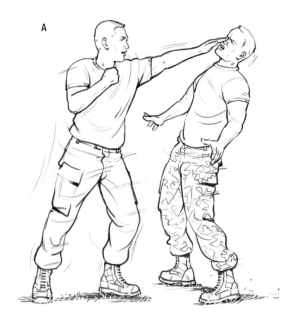

sometimes called 'shut down–put down', i.e. the soldier first 'shuts down' the opponent by not allowing him to do what he intends, then puts him down with a finishing move. There are many options, of which the example that follows is just one.

The soldier opens with a fast eye strike, causing the opponent to flinch and interrupting whatever he was planning to do. The soldier immediately follows up with a palm shot to the head. This will probably not hit the chin as the hostile will have moved his head away from the eye strike, but it will stun him wherever it lands and should drive him back, off balance.

The soldier then lunges forwards and grabs the opponent around the head, jerking him violently forward to prevent him recovering mentally or physically from the attack, and delivers punishing knee strikes to the body. Finally the soldier steps back a pace, dragging the weakened opponent's head down and dumps him hard on his face. If necessary this can be followed up with kicks.

Lead Hand Grab or Punch Defence

Relatively few people can strike effectively with the lead (i.e. weak) hand, but it is always possible to encounter an enemy with the skill and training to do so. More common is a grab with the lead hand, followed up with strikes made with the strong hand. Either way, the opponent is extending a straight arm towards the soldier, creating opportunities to counterattack.

A straight grab or strike is relatively easy to defend against by deflecting it to the side, but it does come in fast, which requires the soldier to be alert and ready to act. At the minimum a straight attack can be batted to the side, causing it to fail. However, more is achieved if the soldier can use the opponent's arm as a lever to turn his whole body. This is not especially difficult if the attacker has fully committed to his action.

Perhaps the simplest option is to break the opponent's arm at the elbow. To do this the soldier steps diagonally forwards to the outside of the arm as it extends towards him, stepping through with his rear foot and turning so that he is facing the opponent's shoulder. The soldier's left arm (assuming the attacker is right-handed and grabbing or striking with his lead, i.e. left, hand) is used to trap the attacker's arm by raising the soldier's forearm vertically from the elbow, which is bent at about 90 degrees. This prevents the arm moving away from the strike delivered by the soldier's right arm. The striking point is close to the elbow and the blow is pushed right through.

Alternatively, the soldier can step in so that he is very close to the opponent's armpit and simply yank the arm towards him, pushing his chest forwards to act as a fulcrum. The resulting levering action will dislocate the opponent's elbow.

For a greater range options the soldier can bring his left hand outside the attack and deflect it by pushing the opponent's arm 'inwards' as he steps diagonally forwards. This turns the opponent away from the soldier whilst placing the soldier facing the opponent's side. From here a knee to the thigh or a body shot to the kidney area are good options, but arguably the best is a hooking elbow strike that lands behind the opponent's ear. This is an excellent knockout blow, though it is problematical if the opponent is wearing a helmet.

Swinging Punch Defence

Most people, trained or otherwise, tend to revert to big swinging strikes when under pressure. These can be hard to stop as they come around a standard guard position, and they hit hard. Fortunately they are relatively slow and are usually 'telegraphed', i.e. it is obvious what the opponent is about to do.

Probably the best defence against a swinging strike is to use a straight lead-hand attack. If both are launched at the same time, the straight shot will get there first. It need not be all that precise; a straight palm shot to the face or forehead will interrupt the opponent's swing and take him off balance. He might still land a weak blow but the soldier can ride that and keep throwing his own shots. For the price of taking a weakened punch (if it lands at all) he will win the fight, which is what matters.

However, this option is not always viable. A hooking or swinging blow can be covered or smothered as discussed in the previous chapter. Another option is to avoid it completely. This could be accomplished by stepping back but that is ultimately pointless. The opponent will simply continue to advance and throw more shots. The answer is, of course, an aggressive defence using the evasion to improve the soldier's position. The following is just one example.

Duck and Hit

As the opponent strikes, the soldier ducks under the blow and moves forwards, delivering a body shot of his own as he does so. This has both combatants' forwards movement to add to its impact; it will go in deep and hard, and the opponent may well double up or stagger. The soldier comes back up on the far side of the opponent's striking arc and is now on his flank. It is worth taking an instant to assess the situation from here – the opponent may be falling, stumbling or otherwise moving in a way that limits the soldier's options.

Now positioned on the opponent's flank, the soldier picks

Grab Defence

Once a grab is anchored firmly there is no point in fiddling about trying to peel it off and apply a wrist lock. Instead the soldier drops his forearm into the crook of the grabbing arm, driving down hard to bend the arm and pull the opponent forwards, onto a counterattack.

This should be done quickly if the opponent is about to
throw a punch, or to cover the head, ride the punch
and then bend the arm to launch a counterattack.

Lead Hand Grab or Punch Defence

Any straight movement of the lead arm can be deflected, creating a chance for a counterattack. It is best to push the arm across the body, placing the soldier 'on the outside' where the opponent's other arm is as far away as possible. This creates the bets chance for a counterattack whilst limiting the opponent's options.

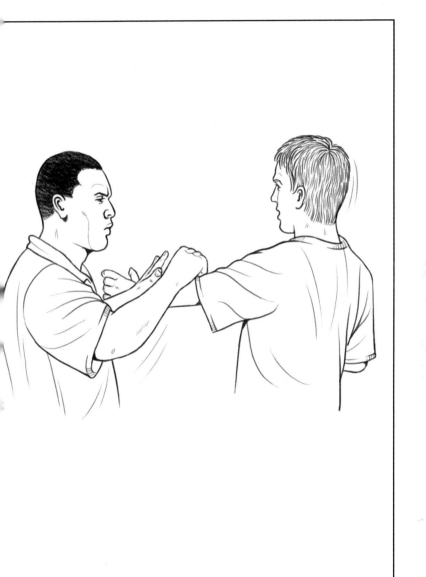

Swinging Punch Defence

A big swinging strike (with or without a weapon in the hand) can be ducked. The soldier bends at the legs and crouches to get under the strike, making sure he keeps looking forwards rather than down. He then snaps back up and delivers a blow of his own as the opponent tries to recover from his missed strike.

a suitable option and makes his attack. A roundhouse kick to the back of the leg will disable the opponent's leg and will likely cause him to topple to the ground. It is also possible to close in with elbow strikes and body shots, smothering the opponent in blows before he can recover.

In the face of a barrage of swinging strikes, it can be difficult to make a very precise response. It is absolutely essential to do something, and to do it immediately, otherwise the soldier will be battered into submission. It is tempting to fold up, turn away or reel backwards in the hope that the attack will stop – but it won't. Here, the fighting spirit is all-important because the only way out of this situation is forwards.

Close and Shut Down

Even if he has been hit and 'rattled' the soldier must close in and shut his opponent down. This means covering the head with the arms and lurching forwards, grabbing the opponent as best he can. If the soldier can 'tie up' his opponent's arms for a moment he can collect his wits and get back into the fight. One good option from this position is the inner reaping takedown. Alternatively, the soldier can hang onto his opponent with one arm and deliver body hooks and elbow strikes until he gains an advantage. His grip can then be 'traded up' for a head

or arm clinch and the opponent finished off with knee strikes or a takedown and stomp.

Kick Defence

The only time a kicking attack is likely is when the soldier is downed. Against a standing target most people will attack with the arms, though a swinging kick, like kicking a football, is possible. Trained personnel might use a simple kick like a front kick; a roundhouse is less likely but might happen. The likelihood of facing a complex martial arts move, such as a jumping and/or spinning kick, is vanishingly small, while many other martial arts kicks are only useful in light-contact point-scoring matches. Even if they do land, such attacks will not stop the soldier demolishing the kicker.

A swinging football-type kick will normally be aimed at the legs or groin, and is defended against in the same way as a front kick. The soldier sidesteps, allowing the opponent's momentum to carry him into range for a counterattack. If the kick is high enough, it can be deflected to the side by sweeping it away with an arm, or it can be caught. This is not in any way the same thing as 'blocking' a kick. Slamming an arm into a leg coming the other way is not an effective way to prevent a determined kick from doing damage.

Deflecting or evading a kick requires that the soldier moves to the

Close and Shut Down

A soldier who has been rocked by a blow is likely to be wide open to follow-ups, which will be heavy, fight-ending shots. To avoid being taken out, he must 'shut down' the threat while he regains his composure.
He covers his head and 'crashes in', grabbing the opponent's striking arm to prevent any more blows being thrown. From here, he can get back in the fight.

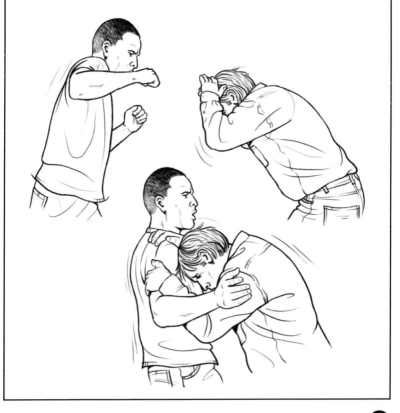

Kick Shield

It is not always possible to predict where a roundhouse kick is going to land, although it is unlikely to be aimed at the head in a fight outside a sporting competition.

The soldier brings up his knee and turns slightly away from the kick, dropping his arm down onto his leg to create a shield all down that side of his body. The kick will hit the shield before it has developed full power.

'outside' of the kick, i.e. is diagonally off to the side afterwards. This has the advantage that if the opponent will not run into the defender if he continues to move forwards with the momentum of his kick.

Deflecting a kick also turns the opponent away from the soldier to some extent, meaning that he has to turn back before making his next attack. He is vulnerable to strikes or a takedown during this time.

Even if the kick has not been deflected but merely dodged there is still a moment where the kicker's weight is falling forwards and he

Special Forces Tip: Recovery before Retaliation

An opponent has to recover from being attacked before he can retaliate. If he is off balance he must regain his base. If he is stunned he must gather his wits. If he is facing the wrong way, he must turn. Continued attacks keep the enemy confused, staggering and unable to respond effectively.

cannot change direction or defend against a counterattack.

Catching a Kick

Catching a kick normally requires that the defender moves to the 'inside' and remains in front of the opponent. This is more risky but does allow a very effective response. If the defender lifts up the opponent's leg and pushes it back towards his face – as if trying to feed him his own knee – then the opponent will topple backwards. For a much harder takedown the soldier steps in close as he lifts the kicker's leg and hooks the supporting leg away with his foot.

A roundhouse kick is harder to defend against. It may be possible to step back out of range then close in fast once the kick has gone past. If not, there are only two good options. One is a 'wall block' or 'shield' as used by Muay Thai fighters. The roundhouse kick is a major part of their fighting system, so they have more experience at defending against it than anyone else. Ideally, the defender moves forwards to shorten the kick's arc and weaken it, and creates a shield by lifting up his leg and covering his head and ribs with his arm. This mitigates the kick but it will still hurt. Fortunately, most roundhouse kick attacks are not all that well performed and are relatively weak. Alternatively, the defender can move diagonally forwards, moving both away from the kick and down its arc to weaken it. The kick will still hurt as it lands but this should be tolerable and it allows the kick to be caught. A takedown can be performed as above, or the defender can throw the opponent's leg in the direction of the kick's rotation, turning his body to add power. This may damage the kicker's knee and will certainly send him to the ground where he is vulnerable.

Grab and Choke Defences

Whilst being grabbed is not usually life-threatening, a soldier or police officer in a combat situation cannot afford to risk being held while another opponent attacks him. Grabs can also be the basis for takedowns or attacks and, of course, it is possible that a hostile might be able to apply a choke or other lethal technique.

In a situation where there are multiple opponents, fixating on escaping from a grab can be dangerous. Obviously if the soldier is being choked then he needs to deal with that as a priority but if he is being held then he must decide whether to work towards getting free or deal with an additional attacker. There is little point in struggling out of a bear hug only to be taken out of the fight by another assailant. It may be a better option to kick out at the new opponent and make some space before trying to get free.

Front Grab Defence

A front grab, e.g. where the opponent takes hold of clothing, is not much of a threat. However, the blows that will surely follow are. The soldier cannot focus on the grab to the extent where he is hit repeatedly. The inwards and outwards wrist locks discussed earlier can be used to dislodge a grab that is not properly secured but an opponent who has taken a solid grip cannot be dealt with in this way; it will take too long, and all the while the soldier will be eating heavy blows to the head.

The best defence against a front grab is to deflect it before it lands or perhaps to use a wrist lock before it

Special Forces Tip: Do Something. Do It Now!

A pause spent trying to figure out the absolute best thing to do is time given to the enemy, so it is better to do the obvious thing straight away, even if it may not be the best possible option. Too late is too late.

Kick Catch and Takedown

As the opponent throws a
straight kick, the soldier
moves slightly to the side
and catches the kick by
looping an arm under the
kicking leg.

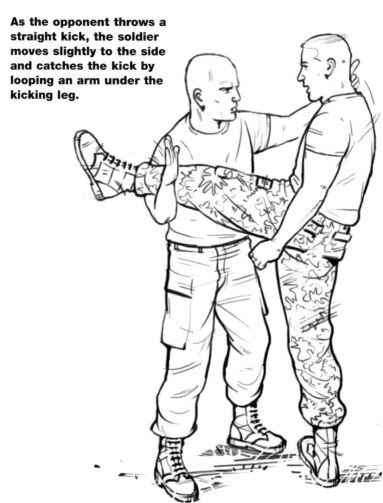

The soldier then steps diagonally forwards and hooks the opponent's other leg away, driving forwards and down with his free arm and lifting up the kicking leg as high as he can. A very hard fall will result.

Roundhouse Kick Catch

The soldier moves either forwards to shorten the kick and diagonally away from it, reducing the force it develops. The arms are also used to jam the kick, taking the force on the upper arm rather than the body. An arm looped under the kicking leg is then

lifted up and dragged in the direction the kick was originally travelling. Simultaneously, the soldier turns in the same direction and 'throws' the leg past him, dumping the opponent to the ground.

is properly in place. Once it is established, the soldier needs to be ready to cover the blow that will be coming, and then to deal with the grab. This is done by pushing a forearm into the crook of the opponent's arm to bend it, pulling him in close. The soldier can then establish a head clinch and deliver knee hits, or strike with his free hand. A web hand strike to the throat is highly effective from this position.

Front Bear Hug Defence

A front bear hug is not that much of a threat – the opponent has tied up

Front Grab Defence

A grab that is not yet properly anchored can be peeled off and a wrist lock applied. However, this will not work if the opponent is landing punches. It is necessary to act before he starts striking, or to cover the strike before peeling off the grab.

most of his limbs and must let go to do anything more serious. However, it can be used to throw the soldier to the ground or bash him into a wall. He is also vulnerable to an attack from the rear.

If his hands are free, i.e. the grip is under his arms, the soldier has the option to secure his release by jamming his thumb into the opponent's eye or throat. The soft cavity to the side of the larynx is a good target; fingers around the side and back of the head will secure the grip in place. Alternatively, the opponent can be peeled off by getting a hand under his chin and pushing it up and back. Driving forwards from this position should make him fall backwards.

A grab over the arms is more of a problem, but not much so. The soldier defends by dropping his weight and splaying his arms, making himself wider and harder to hold. This will give him some space to move his arms. A strike or grab to the testicles is an option from here, or it may be possible to get a hand up the centreline and push the opponent's head back as above.

Rear Bear Hug Defence

A rear bear hug under the arms invites the soldier to grab and break fingers, which tends to quickly secure release. It is also possible to get the opponent to let go by smashing the middle joints of the soldier's fingers

into the back of the opponent's hand. Once the grip has been loosened, the soldier can peel one of the opponent's hands off the other and make a gap. He can then keep hold of this hand as he spins out through the gap, placing him in a good position for a finish.

A rear bear hug over the arms is dealt with in the same way as one from the front. The soldier drops his weight and makes himself wide, then curls his hand up and inside the opponent's grip to peel it off. Again, he spins out through the gap and delivers a finishing strike.

All bear hug defences can be accompanied by front or back headbutts and stomps to the opponent's feet. The target here is the top of the foot close to the ankle, not the toes.

Defending a Tackle

Many opponents will come in with what looks a lot like a rugby tackle. This is an instinctive move for many people; the attacker himself may have no clear idea of what he intends! A tackle can lead to a bear hug or the target being driven backwards; perhaps it might be a deliberate takedown attempt. Whatever the intent, the soldier needs to ensure it does not succeed.

A well-timed knee strike to the head will stop any tackle attempt, but this is risky as failure virtually guarantees going over backwards as

Front Bear Hug Defence

A bear hug crushing the arms to the body leaves few good options, but can be broken by grabbing the opponent's testicles and crushing or twisting them (A). Even if the grab fails, the threat will usually cause an opponent to change his position and weaken his grip.

The soldier then twists his body and works his other arm free, lifting it up the outside and pivoting to that side (B). This applies an arm or shoulder lock, and forces the opponent down (C).

A

B

C

Rear Bear Hug Defence

A bear hug may be over or under the arms. If they are free, it is usually possible to secure release by breaking the opponent's fingers. To escape from an over-arms bear hug the soldier drops his weight and pushes his upper arms out, then reaches over to peel one of the opponent's hands free.

Over arm bear hug

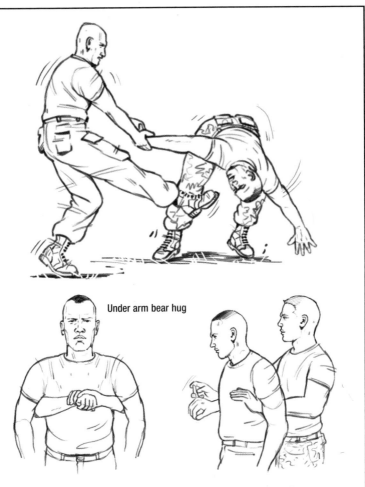

Under arm bear hug

He 'spins out' through the gap thus made, holding the opponent's arm as he steps out and round. This may give him an arm lock or drive the opponent's head down where it can be easily kicked.

the assailant drives in. A better option is to step back and use a variant of the 'faceplant' takedown from a head clinch. The soldier drops his hands heavily onto the back of the opponent's head or neck as he steps back; the attacker's own momentum will drive him face-first into the ground.

If the tackle does connect, the soldier must get a foot well behind

Defending a Tackle

Moving back and driving the opponent's head down is an excellent way to deal with a tackle (A). Alternatively a 'sprawl' as used by mixed martial artists can be performed. The soldier skips both feet well back, allowing his weight to fall on the opponent's back (B). The opponent is then driven face-first into the ground by the combined weight of both combatants (C).

A

him. This not only prevents him being pushed back or tipped over backwards, but it keeps that leg out of reach of the attacker. If he can grab both of the soldier's legs he can execute a double-leg takedown as seen in many martial arts competitions. This causes a very heavy fall that may well take the soldier out of the fight. If there

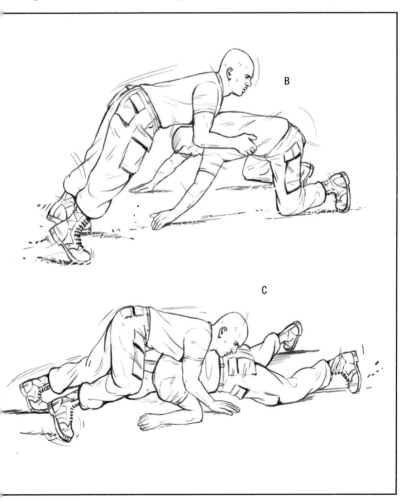

B

C

Jamming a Tackle

The soldier stops himself being tipped over backwards by getting one leg well behind him, and pushes down on the opponent's back or head. From here he can drop hammerfists or elbow strikes into the opponent's back or perhaps loop his free arm around the opponent's neck for a standing choke.

is any danger of the opponent
getting hold of both legs, the
soldier must 'sprawl', jumping
backwards with both legs and
falling forwards so that his weight
drives the attacker face down into
the ground, with the soldier on top.

In the case of a failed tackle, the
soldier may end up with an opponent
gripping him around the waist and/or
one or both legs and trying to upend
him. A good 'base', i.e. a solid stance
with the feet well apart, will help
prevent this but the attacker must still
be dealt with. Ramming an elbow
into the back under the shoulder
blade will weaken him or,
alternatively, hammerfists can be
delivered to the lung area with the
same effect. Hopefully the opponent
will be sufficiently hurt that he will
lose his grip and slide down to land
at the soldier's feet. If not, he will
have to be dislodged.

Trying to bring a knee up to strike
at this point is inadvisable because it
compromises the soldier's balance.
Instead, the attacker is peeled off
sideways. The soldier places one
hand on top of the opponent's
shoulder and forces his opposite arm
under the opponent's arm, bringing
his hand up. As he lifts on that side,
he pushes down on the other and
rotates as if performing one of the
clinch takedowns discussed in the
previous chapter. This action wheels
him to the ground where he can be
easily finished off.

Defending a Headlock
Another common occurrence in
fights is the headlock. This often
happens by accident as a natural
consequence of grabbing and
wrestling for a good position,
though it is sometimes deliberately
used. A good headlock also applies
a choke or strangle in addition to
leaving the target open to strikes,
and must be dislodged as quickly
as possible.

A testicle grab or strike will often
secure release. If not, the best way
out is to reach up and back and jam
the edge of the hand into the
opponent's face between his nose
and mouth. This area, the philtrum,
is extremely sensitive and pressure
there will cause the opponent to
straighten up to get away from the
pain. The soldier straightens with him,
placing a foot behind the opponent's
and sweeping it away. This dumps
the opponent on his back.

If the opponent has secured a good
choke then it may be necessary to
loosen it before attempting an escape.
This is a matter of getting hold of the
choking arm and pulling it down using
both hands. Once it is loosened then
the choke can be held off with one
hand while the other secures release
from the hold as above.

Defending a Rear Choke
A rear choke is defended in a
similar way. It is loosened by
pulling it down and off, allowing

the soldier to get his chin in behind the opponent's arm and prevent the choke being reapplied. It may also be possible to turn the head into the crook of the opponent's arm, which creates a space to breathe. From here, it is possible to work towards making an escape.

It is virtually impossible to wriggle out of a choke in which the soldier is bent backwards, so an essential part of the defence is to bend forwards as much as possible. Stomps to the feet and backwards elbows and headbutts can all help make it difficult for the opponent to hang on, enabling the soldier to pull the choking arm away from his throat and escape from the hold.

Ideally he will make enough of a gap to spin out, much as with a bear hug, but it may only be possible to turn awkwardly around whilst still held by the opponent. This is a much better position; the soldier cannot be choked to death from here, but there is still work to do to escape.

Defend to Win

Knee strikes, thumbs driven into the eyes or throat, and pushing the head up and back will create a space. Once he has obtained room to counterattack, the soldier must do so vigorously until the opponent is disabled. Getting the choke off is only a start; what comes next is winning the fight.

Defending a Rear Choke

It is possible to pull a choke off or to grab fingers and break them, but once the choke is properly locked in this becomes impossible. It is thus necessary to act fast and avoid being bent backwards by hunching forwards as much as possible.

7

Leaving aside firearms for the moment, there are three basic types of hand weapon: stabbing, cutting and blunt. Weapons are effective only when used correctly. A stabbing weapon must be pushed into the body; a cutting weapon can only do so if it moves in contact with flesh. A blunt weapon needs to move to gain momentum.

Some weapons can do more than one of these things, e.g. a commando knife can be used to stab or cut. It is not much use for bludgeoning, however, so a soldier who sees such a knife in the hands of an opponent knows that he faces a stabbing or a cutting attack, which is a starting point for his defence.

There are two very basic principles to dealing with an armed opponent. Firstly, it is the user, not the weapon, that is the threat. Disarming a knife-wielding opponent is not a 'win' if he fights on unarmed; he can still deliver a beating or regain his weapon. Take out the user, on the other hand, and the weapon becomes inert. Secondly, a weapon that is held immobile cannot do any damage unless someone falls on it or moves onto the point or blade. Some defences

....

Bladed, pointed and impact weapons each pose a different kind of threat. Recognizing the weapon type allows the opponent's actions to be somewhat predictable.

The Armed Opponent

Law Enforcement Tip: Dangerous Weapons?

A weapon increases the user's capabilities, but a lethal weapon in the hands of a pacifist is less dangerous than an unarmed psychopath. What matters most is the user's intent, not the potential of the weapon.

Controlling the Weapon

A blunt weapon needs momentum to cause damage, which usually requires that it be swung in an arc.

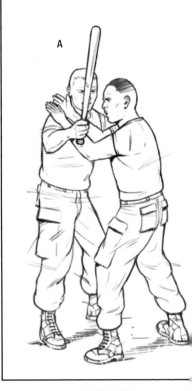

A

hold the weapon in a position where it cannot do any harm, whilst the attacker is dealt with. This is a better option than fixating on disarming the opponent rather than taking him out of the fight.

Blunt Weapon Defences

Most blunt (or crushing) weapons resemble sticks of various lengths. Deliberately fashioned clubs, baseball bats, chair legs and the like are all basically clubs. Other blunt weapons may be awkwardly shaped but can still deliver massive impact. These include rifle butts, fire extinguishers, a rock or can of food held in the hand or virtually any object with heft. It is possible (and surprisingly

If the soldier can get inside the arc and 'jam' the swing (A) in exactly the same way a hooked punch he can then trap the weapon arm (B). The opponent still has hold of his weapon, but it is under control and cannot do any harm (C).

effective) to use a blunt weapon to jab with rather than swinging it. Such attacks can often be treated as a stab (see below). It is also conceivable, though unlikely, that an opponent might use a blunt weapon to apply chokes or joint locks. This requires a lot of training, however, and is best defended against by not allowing him to try, i.e. by an aggressive attack that nullifies his fancy techniques.

Thus most of the time a soldier faces one of two or perhaps three attacks – the forehand swing, backhand swing, and straight down. Some opponents will wave a weapon around as a threat, chambering it as if to make one of these attacks but not actually doing it. This is dealt with by an aggressive attack.

Defending a Forehand Swing

Faced with a forehand swing, the soldier has a couple of good options. One is to duck under the swing and use a sideways stomping kick to the side of the opponent's knee. This will not disarm him, but it will render him incapable of fighting or even standing, which is a better result.

Alternatively, the soldier can close in and jam the attack as if it were a swinging punch (it follows a very similar path). He then wraps the opponent's weapon arm to immobilize the weapon and executes either a reaping takedown or repeated hand or knee strikes.

Avoiding the Weapon

Ducking under the swing avoids it but does not give the soldier control of the weapon. However, his stomping kick to the side of the knee will probably put the opponent out of the fight, which makes control unnecessary. A baseball bat is not much of a threat in the hands of someone who cannot stand up.

Defending a Forehand Swing

As the opponent swings his weapon, the soldier steps inside the weapon's arc and jams the swing, looping his arm over and round the weapon arm to trap it. He then delivers a series of short, hard, strikes to the opponent's head as he struggles to free his arm.

Defending a Backhand Swing

A backhand strike can be jammed by pushing the opponent's arm or elbow back towards him while the strike is chambered or just beginning to move. The soldier then reaches over the opponent's shoulder with his free hand and grabs the weapon, pulling it forwards to apply a painful and difficult to escape headlock. This can be used to rotate the opponent to the ground or to hold him for knee strikes followed by a faceplant takedown.

Defending an Overhead Swing

The soldier steps out from under the weapon's arc rather than trying to block it directly (A).

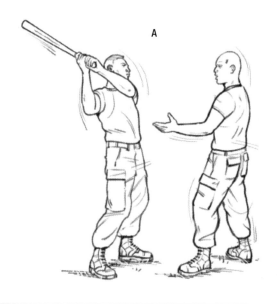

A

Defending An Overhead Strike

Against a direct overhead attack, usually executed with a heavy weapon requiring both hands, the soldier steps forward and out to either side on the Tactical 'Y', turning to face the attacker. He helps the weapon on its way by slapping the attacker's hands downwards as they go past, which will cause him to tip forwards off balance. The weapon will probably strike the ground and can be trapped by pushing down on one of the

He pushes the opponent's arms down as the strike goes past, making it harder to recover from the missed strike (B). While the opponent is still off balance the soldier then delivers a low roundhouse kick to the back of the legs (C).

Defending a Backhand Swing

As the opponent winds up for his swing, the soldier lunges in and pushes the striking arm back to jam the swing (A).

A

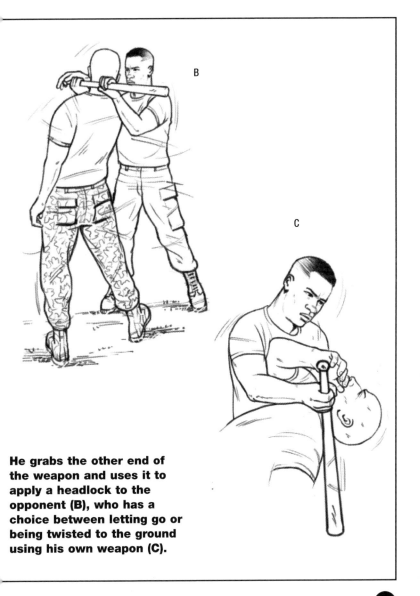

He grabs the other end of the weapon and uses it to apply a headlock to the opponent (B), who has a choice between letting go or being twisted to the ground using his own weapon (C).

attacker's arms while the soldier delivers a barrage of strikes.

Sharp and/or Pointed Weapon Defences

As a general rule, slashing attacks tend to be aimed at the head and neck, and stabbing attacks at the abdomen or side of the torso. A trained knifeman may slash at other locations, such as the femoral artery in the legs or the tendons of the arms, but this is less likely than a simple slash or grab-and-stab.

Ideally the soldier will be able to pre-empt the attack, perhaps before the weapon is even drawn. Some people are adept at concealing knives, but if at any time during a confrontation a hand goes 'out of play', i.e. it goes into a pocket or under clothing instead of remaining ready to strike or guard with then it is certain that a weapon is about to be produced.

It may be possible to take the opponent out of the fight as he reaches for his weapon. A determined attack may overwhelm him while he is occupied in deploying his knife or other implement. If not, then the soldier will have to deal with an armed attack. It will not be possible to merely defend; this opponent must be taken out of the fight swiftly and decisively.

A stabbing attack is likely to be a single attempt only if there is a heavy weapon in play, such as a bayonet on the end of a rifle. A knife is more likely to be used for repeated stabs, often accompanied by a grab. The fanciful disarms and hopelessly optimistic 'X-blocks' of many martial arts are of no use in either case. The soldier must instead get past the point of the weapon and defeat the user.

One-Handed Stab

A one-handed stab can be swept aside using the outside of the arm (a cut here will not be life-threatening, if it happens at all) while the soldier steps diagonally forwards along the Tactical 'Y'. From an 'outside' position such as this, it is possible to break the arm holding the knife, as discussed under grabs earlier, or to execute a disarming manoeuvre. The

Law Enforcement Tip: Watch the Hands!

If a potential opponent's hands go out of sight, they're coming back with a weapon. The time to act is while he is still reaching for it, not when it's coming right at you!

Kicks and Sharp Weapons

Kicking someone who is using a knife or similar weapon can be an effective way to create an opening to get close enough to control the weapon. Trying to kick the weapon away is very little short of suicide.

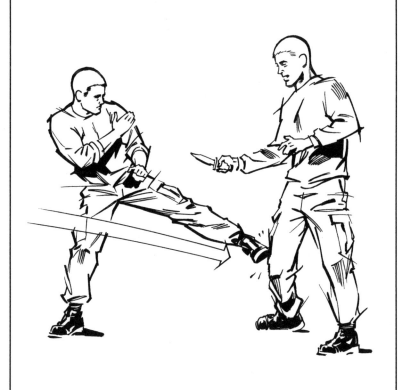

Knife Defence

It is necessary to control the weapon as much as possible. By placing himself 'behind' the weapon arm and pushing it down, the soldier has made it impossible for the opponent to stab him while he delivers a knee strike. This control is temporary, however; if the opponent withstands the strike he still has a lethal implement to fight with so the soldier must follow up rapidly.

Special Forces Tip: No Fancy Stuff!

Kicking knives and even guns out of people's hands looks good on television and in the movies. Unfortunately that's the only place it works.

soldier steps in so that his hip is close to the opponent's armpit and wrenches the arm towards him, perhaps breaking it. From here he can fold the attacker's wrist and strip the knife out of his hand. Elbow strikes can also be delivered to the back of the attacker's head.

An 'inside' position is more problematical as it is easier for the knifeman to attack from here. The soldier may be able to snake the attacker's arm and thus immobilize the knife, or push the elbow back to control the weapon. Web-hand strikes to the throat are a good follow-up. The knifeman may try to retreat in order to clear his weapon and attack again. He must not be allowed to do so but must be taken swiftly out of the fight.

Bayonet Attack

Against a bayonet attack, similar options can be used. It is possible to snake the rifle from an inside position, just like an arm. In this position, the muzzle and its attached bayonet are pointed away from the

soldier so he cannot be shot or stabbed. From an outside position, the attacker's arm can be struck in the hope of bending the elbow the wrong way, breaking it. The arm is then pulled towards the soldier, forcing his head down. A kick to the head is an option from here, or the enemy can be driven face-first into the ground.

Slashing Attack

A slashing attack is less likely to result in fatality but is harder to defend against. With a stab, the attack is dangerous only along a narrow line out from the tip of the weapon. A slash is dangerous anywhere on the weapon's arc.

A forehand slash can be jammed in the same way as a hook punch. It is vital to immobilize the arm and to prevent the opponent pulling away to make another attack. He will almost certainly fixate on trying to regain control of his weapon, and while his attention is on trying to pull it free the soldier has an opportunity to win the fight. In an extreme close-

Bayonet Stab Defence

With any stabbing attack, the weapon will move directly towards the target (A). By stepping to the side and deflecting the weapon the soldier creates an opportunity to counterattack (B). He seizes the opponent's arm and attempts an arm break (C), using pressure on the arm to push his opponent's head down (D). A kick to the face should take him out of the fight (E).

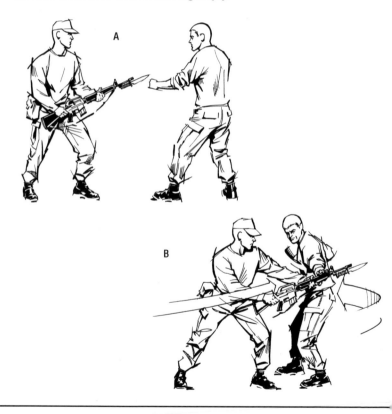

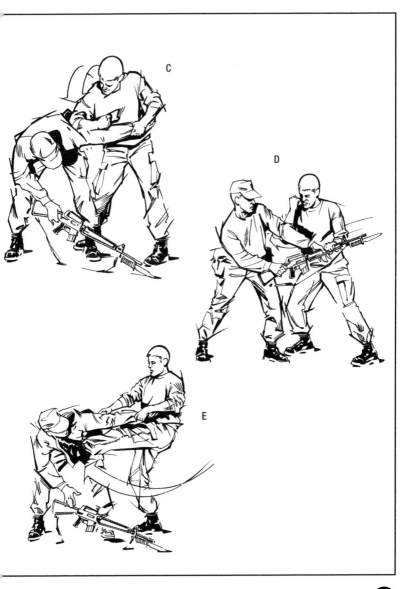

Stabbing Attack

A stabbing attack is deflected to the side rather than being 'blocked' head-on (A). If the knife is deflected to the outside so that the soldier is still directly in front of the opponent, a direct striking counterattack is the best option (B). If the deflection places the soldier to the outside of the opponent's arm, he has more options including an arm break or disarming technique (C), or a counterstrike (D).

A

B

C

D

Forehand Slashing Attack

A slash follows a path similar to a swinging punch and can be jammed by stopping the attacker's arm. A web-hand strike to the throat is an effective counterattack from this position.

quarters situation involving a weapon, any measure is justified.

Biting the attacker may distract him from fighting for the knife, allowing telling strikes to be delivered. Alternatively, a thumb in his eye socket will cause him to pull his head back. Avoiding damage to the eye will be momentarily more important to him than trying to work his knife hand free.

During this time the soldier might headbutt the opponent in the nose, knee him or set up a takedown. It is vital to keep the knife immobilized during a takedown and after hitting the ground, and to deal with the opponent with the utmost savagery. If the knife comes free at any point, then the soldier is likely to be killed.

A backhand swipe almost always follows a forehand one. This can be jammed by pushing the opponent's arm against his body, or better by seizing him in a hug that pins the knife against him. From here it is possible to take him down and keep the knife pinned, finishing him with blows to the head.

In a military context, few opponents will use a knife as a threat – soldiers are rarely mugged in a war zone. However, an enemy might threaten with a knife to avoid capture or to try to take a soldier captive. Law enforcement officers may be threatened with knives or attacked with them as they try to make an arrest.

If the knife is a short way in front of the soldier (as opposed to being in contact with him) them the usual counter is a two-handed blow that strikes the back of the hand and the inside of the wrist. This folds the knifeman's wrist and may send his weapon flying away.

If it does not then at least it redirects the weapon so that it is no longer pointed at the target, who can then close in and follow up. Alternatively the soldier can push the knife to the side and launch a barrage of strikes.

Knife to Throat Threat

A knife held against the throat (from the front or behind) is a very serious threat. From the rear, it can be pulled down and held away from the throat while the soldier rolls his shoulder forwards and down. This executes a shoulder throw on the opponent, dumping him on the ground where he can be finished off. The weapon must be immobilized throughout.

From the front, it is vital to recognize which way the weapon is pointing. Pushing it the wrong way will cut the soldier's throat. Once the weapon's orientation is noted, the soldier will attempt a distraction, perhaps begging for mercy, to put the opponent off his guard. The knife is then pushed aside in an explosive movement and the soldier steamrollers his opponent before he can recover.

Backhand Slashing Attack

A backhand slash can be jammed by pushing the opponent's arm against his body. This immobilizes the weapon long enough to launch a counterattack. Pressure must be maintained, however; the opponent will try to step back to clear his weapon.

Frontal Knife Threat

Striking the back of the hand and the wrist simultaneously may send the weapon flying out of the opponent's hand. Even if it does not, it will fold the wrist and point the weapon in a less threatening direction. This buys time for a follow-up attack.

Knife to Throat Threat

It is absolutely vital to prevent the knife from cutting, so it must be immobilized or held away from the throat throughout any defence. The soldier achieves this by pulling the knife arm down and away from his throat (B), then rolls his shoulder forwards and down (C), dragging the opponent over to fall heavily in front of him (D and E). Finishing strikes to the head are then delivered (F). The knife arm is held throughout.

A

B

8

A nyone, armed or otherwise, who faces a firearm in the hands of someone willing to use it is in severe danger. Tackling a weapon whilst unarmed is one of the most difficult things a soldier or law enforcement officer could be asked to do. Yet if it becomes necessary, he does stand a chance provided he acts with intensity and resolve.

Tackling a Gunman

Firearms are extremely loud and become hot when they are fired. This can cause someone who has grabbed a gun to let go if it goes off. It is necessary to hang on even if the weapon is hot, because letting go allows the gunman free use of it. A firearm that is pulled forwards is likely to discharge as the forwards movement effectively pulls the trigger. It is thus vital to be out of the line of fire at all times.

An assailant's finger on the trigger can be an asset when trying to disarm him, as twisting the weapon

· ·

Some firearms make fairly decent unarmed combat weapons, especially when combined with a bayonet. However, for the unarmed soldier the only option is to close in and either gain control of the weapon or take the user out of the fight. If the soldier is out of touching range, an armed opponent has all the advantages.

Firearms can only shoot in the direction they are pointing. The key to all successful firearm defences is to ensure that the weapon is never pointing at you.

Firearms

Bodyguard Tip: Guns are Loud!

People who may have to face firearms, such as bodyguards, train with blank-firing guns to get used to the noise when one discharges. It is normal to flinch in the face of sudden noise, and a bodyguard fighting for a gun cannot afford to do so.

may break his finger or at least cause intense pain that will force him to let go. The weapon can also be caused to malfunction. For example, if a semi-automatic pistol fires while someone has hold of the slide (the top part of the weapon that surrounds the barrel and moves back and forth to eject a spent round and chamber the next) it may fail to feed and 'jam'. This will render it inoperable until the malfunction has been cleared.

Thus it is not always wise to assume that a weapon taken away from a gunman can be used against him or his allies. Many weapons have safety catches that must be correctly operated for the weapon to fire, and some users carry their weapon uncocked or without a round chambered (or both). Well-trained personnel can render a captured weapon ready to fire in the same movement as bringing it to bear, but for those unused to handling firearms the chance of the weapon not firing is significant. It is a safer bet to club the gunman with his weapon, taking whatever steps are necessary to ready it for use once the immediate threat has been nullified.

Obviously, guns outrange hand-to-hand combat techniques. However, most gunmen, even trained soldiers, cannot shoot accurately under the stress of close combat. A rapidly moving target, even at fairly short range, is hard to hit. Thus it may be possible for the soldier to take advantage of a distraction and bolt for cover. He should not run in a straight line, and ideally should try to get objects in between him and the gunman.

Taking Cover

Taking cover is, of course, an option, but only up to a point. It is important to understand the difference between concealment and cover. Cover is defined as an obstruction that will stop a bullet whereas concealment will not. It will, however, make targeting difficult and may enable the soldier to break contact and escape.

Getting behind some good solid cover will protect against shots fired at the soldier, but there may be nothing to stop the gunman from moving round to where he can get a clear shot, or keeping the soldier pinned down while he closes in for the kill. Thus an escape must be complete or it will fail completely. Entering cover may work if friendly troops can engage the gunman – in this case the soldier only need survive until his comrades deal with the threat.

If this is not the case, then the soldier needs to make his escape. That will normally require breaking contact by getting out of sight and then slipping away or else hiding until the enemy loses interest in searching for him. He may end up hiding until an opportunity arises to ambush one of his pursuers and obtain his weapon, or until the threat is driven off by friendlies entering the area.

Neutralizing the Gunman

If it is not possible to break contact, then the soldier must neutralize the gunman. This can only be done from in close. He will have to choose whether to take his chances on a dash for cover or to attack the gunman. If he is able to launch an ambush or sneak up close, then this is not altogether different from a pre-emptive attack situation. If, on the other hand, the soldier faces a 'gun threat' situation, this is likely to be an attempt to take him prisoner or hostage. His only advantages are that the gunman does not want to immediately shoot him – if he did then he would have already done so – and that he is likely to be held at gunpoint, i.e. very close range. This facilitates a reversal of the situation, albeit only at grave risk of being shot.

There is no possible way to move faster than a gunman's trigger finger. He must simply squeeze the trigger in the same length of time that the soldier has to get his whole body out of the line of fire. Yet it is possible to deal with a gun. This is because there is more to shooting than pulling a trigger. The gunman must observe what the soldier is doing, interpret it as a threatening movement, make the decision to shoot, then pull the trigger. This takes a short time, but that can be enough.

The key is for the soldier to have as much of a head start as possible. If he makes his intentions obvious ('telegraphs' them), e.g. by dropping into a crouch, making a noise, taking a deep breath etc, then he will fail and be shot. On the other hand, if the gunman's first warning that something is happening is the soldier's action then he must run though the whole observation–decision–action sequence while the soldier is already moving. Although the gunman's

Tackling a Sentry

The soldier gets as close as he can without being detected, then launches his attack from behind (A). As he rushes up, his lead arm is ready to grab and his strong hand to strike. He chops his lead hand back into the sentry's throat and strikes him in the back to bend him backwards (B), then puts his hand over the sentry's mouth while continuing to drag him backwards (C).

A

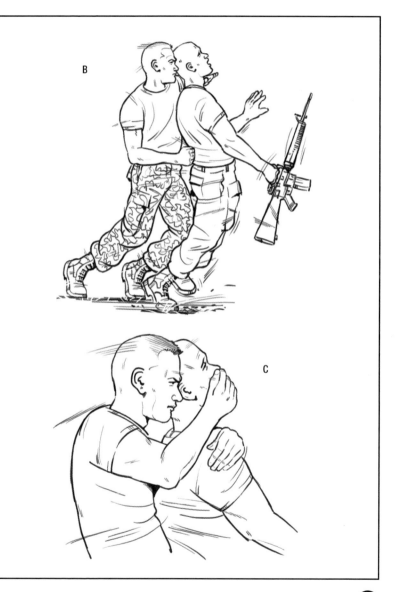

B

C

Weapon Disarm

Twisting a weapon out of the hand is a common component of military disarming techniques. Once the wrist reaches the limit of its movement the weapon can be levered free. In this case the weapon is gripped by the barrel, ensuring that it does not point in a dangerous direction.

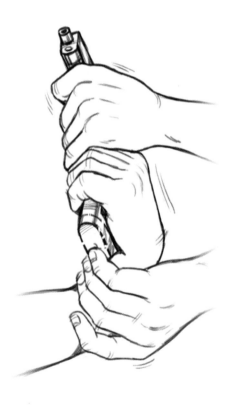

Rifle Threat

The soldier uses his lead hand to deflect the weapon as it is nearest and thus fastest (A). He only has to move it a little to the side to ensure he cannot be shot. He wraps his arm around the weapon behind the muzzle, immobilizing it (B), and attacks the opponent with a groin strike (C).

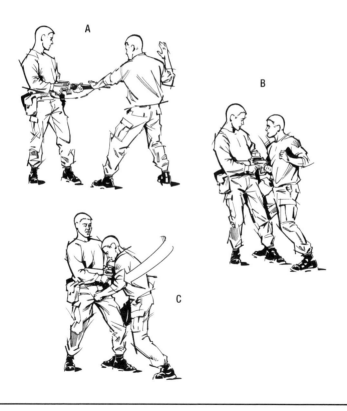

response does not take long to execute, he is already behind. Hopefully this will be enough.

Concealed Intentions

Facing a weapon in front of him, the soldier conceals his intentions by raising his hands to about shoulder-height. This is a typical response to an armed threat and may be exactly what the gunman just told him to do, so it will not raise suspicion. The soldier does not move suddenly or jerkily in case he startles the gunman and causes him to reflexively pull the trigger.

The soldier may try to distract the gunman by saying something – agreeing to comply and surrender, begging for mercy or babbling about his wife, family and household pets back home.

When he moves, he moves suddenly. He swats the gun to one side and lunges in. With a long gun, such as a rifle, the aim is to get 'past' the muzzle. The weapon's own length will prevent the user turning to point it at the soldier. The gunman is now at a disadvantage because he cannot relinquish his weapon and cannot use it. He needs to open some space to start shooting, and the soldier will not let him do that.

Arm Wrap

It may be possible to wrap an arm around the weapon or one (sometimes even both) of the arms holding it, at which point the soldier keeps the gun immobilized while he attacks the gunman with the utmost savagery.

Bites, headbutts, knees and strikes can all be used to subdue the gunman and take away his weapon. If a rifle can be pulled out of its user's hands, it will make a good club with which to finish him off.

A shorter weapon, such as a handgun, can be twisted in the user's hand or tipped back to point at his face. This will discourage him from trying to shoot, to say the least. The usual technique is to

Bodyguard Tip: Secure the Weapon!

Never leave a weapon lying around even after dealing with the user. Make it safe, stash it somewhere inaccessible, or keep possession of it for your own use ... but never leave it lying where a hostile can grab it.

move to the side, out of the line of fire, and push the web of the hand up under the weapon close to the trigger guard. Rotating the hand as if trying to point the thumb at the gunman's face will tip his weapon upwards and ultimately point it at his own head.

Coming from the side rather than underneath the weapon, ideally the soldier's weak hand will go over the top of the weapon, thumb underneath, allowing him to twist it around and bring it to his strong hand. As his weak hand places the gun into his strong one, the soldier can work the slide to ensure a round is chambered, readying the weapon.

More commonly, movements of this nature succeed only partially. The weapon is pushed to the side and the soldier can close in, delivering a series of blows whilst keeping control of the weapon as best he can.

The need to attack and ultimately win must be balanced against the imperative never to allow the weapon to come to point at the soldier. If a situation presents itself where the weapon can be 'stripped' out of the gunman's hand or otherwise removed from his possession, then this is worth doing.

Overall, though, the aim is to keep the weapon pointed in a non-threatening direction whilst demolishing the user.

Rear Threat

Against a rear threat it is necessary to know where the weapon is. A slight turn of the head and use of peripheral vision can work, and a weapon poked into the back gives away its own location. Again, the soldier needs to act abruptly and fast, concealing his intentions for as long as possible. Hands are likely to be raised in this situation; this facilitates the defence.

When he is ready to act, the soldier turns and knocks the weapon aside. If the threat is high, i.e. the gun is pointed at the back of the soldier's head, he keeps his hands high to find it. A low threat (the gun is poked in the back) necessitates bringing down the arms. Precision is not necessary in either case; sweeping a firearm through the general area where the gun is located will push it aside. Speed is, of course, vital.

Depending on which way he turns the soldier may find himself 'inside' or 'outside' the weapon's position. On the inside, the best option is to snake the weapon arm and deliver chinjabs or web-hand strikes to the throat. On the outside, an arm break and/or disarm is best. This is the same movement used for knives and to defend both grabs and punches; the only difference is that the weapon is twisted out of the gunman's hand

High Rear Handgun Threat

The soldier turns suddenly, knocking the weapon aside and controlling it by wrapping the weapon arm with his own. The muzzle is past him and thus not an immediate threat (B). He follows up with an elbow strike to the face, tipping the opponent's head back and unbalancing him (C), and hooks away his foot (D). Still keeping the weapon immobilized he uses a knee-drop onto the opponent's body and delivers strikes to the head (E).

A

B

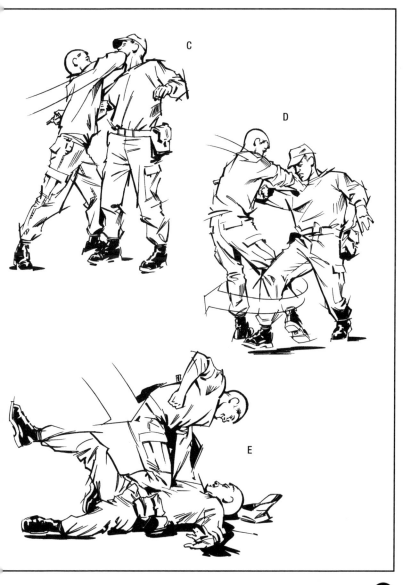

C

D

E

Low Rear Handgun Threat (High-Hand Position)

The soldier turns and sweeps his arm across his body, moving the weapon aside (A). It is immobilized by wrapping the arm (B). The soldier follows up any way he can. In this example he attacks the eyes, breaking the opponent's balance and tipping his head back (C). This exposes the groin to a knee strike.

A

B

C

Low Rear Handgun Threat (Low-Hand Position)

The soldier turns and sweeps the weapon away, but cannot immediately control the weapon arm as his arm is not well positioned (B). Instead he drives forwards and strikes the opponent in the head (C), keeping the weapon pointed away from him by pushing it with his other hand until he can either get the weapon arm under control or the opponent falls unconscious.

A

B

C

9

One person cannot really fight several opponents at once. It is necessary to keep some occupied while one is dealt with, then move on to the next.

Multiple Combatants

One-on-one encounters are rare, other that a situation where an infiltrator attempts to eliminate a lone sentry. More often, the soldier will be engaged with a group of opponents or in a confused melee with several people on each side. In this case, there is no great likelihood that each combatant will single out a suitable opponent. Even if numbers are equal, it is more likely that one soldier will find himself fending off three or four hostiles while his squadmates gang up on lone opponents.

Done deliberately, this tactic can end a fight quickly. If some members of one side can occupy the attentions of a greater number of hostiles then their comrades should, in theory, gain an advantage over the rest.

This will allow some of the enemy personnel to be quickly eliminated from the equation before the remainder are finished off by superior numbers. Of course, this is a two-edged sword; those who are outnumbered need to survive until help arrives or nothing will have been achieved.

....

The only advantage a single soldier has against a group is that they might get in one another's way. Good tactics, such as pushing one into another or causing an opponent to fall where the other will have to move around him, can greatly reduce the odds.

Reducing the Odds

The same tactics for occupying or dealing with a superior number of opponents can be used by the lone soldier facing two or more hostiles, or by a group seeking to neutralize some of the opposition while the rest are demolished.

This principle, known as concentration of force, is an integral part of military strategy. It is not necessary to win everywhere at the same time, only at the decisive point. If one of the enemy goes down while all of the friendlies are still fighting, an advantage is gained. This should lead to a gradual tipping of the balance as more hostiles are taken out by increasingly superior numbers.

For the lone soldier, it is not possible to do anything but concentrate force; he cannot be in several places at once. However, it is possible to prevent the opposition concentrating against him. This is vital because it is not really possible to fight several people at once. What is possible to fight several people one at a time in rapid succession, perhaps switching between opponents as opportunities present themselves.

The lone or outnumbered soldier cannot afford to fixate on one opponent to the point where others can take advantage. He must obtain the absolute maximum result from each action, and he must stay on his feet and keep moving. It is fairly easy for a group to prevent a single person from getting up and to deliver kicks or stomps.

The odds can be temporarily evened by moving so the opponents get in one another's way, or by pushing them into one another. This is sometimes referred to as 'stringing the fish', i.e. getting the opponents lined up rather than surrounding the soldier. It is relatively easy to do with two

Special Forces Tip: What It's Like

There is a lot of back-and-forth in movie fights and sporting bouts. That tends not to happen in real, serious combat. It's more like someone being hit by a car – one side has the advantage and keeps it unless they do something stupid. The other guy isn't given a chance to even get into the fight, let alone win it. The key is to be the car, not the pedestrian.

Reducing the Odds

Few people will walk right over a friend to attack an enemy. By putting one opponent down and using him as a barrier, the soldier can keep his comrades at a distance while he makes his next move.

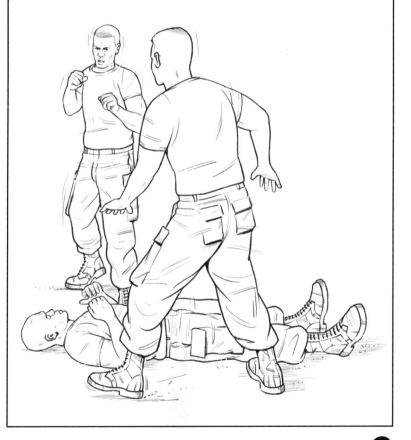

Evening the Odds

Rather than strike the nearest opponent, the soldier pushes him into his comrade. This creates space for a kick that will take him out of the fight and send the remaining opponent reeling. The odds are now more even.

hostiles and becomes progressively harder as numbers increase. Obstacles can also be used to prevent some members of a group closing in.

There are numerous ways to make hostiles impede one another. Stepping to the side so that one is in the way of another is the most obvious. Pushing, or grabbing and turning, one of the hostiles to deliberately place him in the way also works. An opponent can be held in a choke hold and used as a human shield, and a downed opponent makes an effective barrier.

Few people will walk right over a friend or comrade to launch an attack. They will normally step around him, which takes a little time. If the soldier can keep a downed enemy between him and some of his opponents he can deal with others. He may be much more willing to step on the downed enemy than his comrades are; if so, then the soldier can gain the advantage of surprise by charging over a downed enemy, stomping on him in the process, to attack a hostile who has hesitated to do the same thing.

It is also possible to use the distress of an injured enemy to distract his allies. Striking the eyes or throat, or breaking a limb, will often cause at least some of the enemy combatant's associates to try to assist him – or hesitate in case they get the same treatment.

Fighting a Group

The lone soldier facing a group has only one advantage – desperation. Each of his opponents does not have all that much at stake. They can back off and let the others take the risks, relying on the group as a whole to win the fight rather than making the maximum individual effort.

In any group there will be one or two leaders, some who are willing to take risks and get stuck in, and some who want to hang back and stay safe. These individuals will often be quite willing to deliver a beating once someone else has done the work, but if the leaders or the fighters of the group are getting pummelled then these watchers will sometimes just fade away.

The lone fighter cannot rely on anyone else; he must go all-out and make everything he does count. This creates a situation where any given hostile may decide to back off after taking a blow that the lone fighter would have to simply accept and keep on going. It is thus easier to put any given member of a group out of the fight – temporarily or permanently – than it is to take out the lone fighter. Conversely, of course, there are far more fists and feet available to the other side.

Always Attack
The lone fighter must attack. He cannot afford to be grabbed or taken to the ground. Nor can he be

defensive against one opponent while there is another lining up an attack. Each of his movements or attacks must gain him some advantage, though this does not necessarily mean that everything he does must be a massive blow to an opponent's head. It may well be of more value to push one opponent away than to hit him if this allows the lone fighter to deal with another hostile and then come back to the first.

Switch Targets

The lone fighter must be willing to change targets frequently, even if he is on the verge of taking a given opponent right out of the fight. For example, he might push one hostile away and begin unloading a barrage of blows into his comrade. The target is reeling and could be finished off in just another two or three seconds, but there is an unengaged opponent somewhere behind the soldier. He does not win if he batters one into submission and is then taken out by the other. So instead he must turn back to the hostile he pushed and deal with him. Hopefully the other opponent is too badly injured to rejoin the fight (or to want to!) but even if he is still willing and able, the soldier has gained some time to deal with the second opponent before returning to the first. He may have to shuttle back and forth several times, which is inefficient but less likely to result in being attacked from behind.

Techniques used when fighting a group are much the same as one-on-one, but grappling should be avoided. Instead the soldier should use strikes, knees, kicks and pushes to both harm the opponents and move them around. A strike that does little damage but causes the target to recoil at least buys the soldier some time to deal with someone else.

Fighting as Part of a Group

The other side of the multiple-opponent coin is when the soldier has a chance to assist a comrade or gang up on a lone enemy. Teamwork is essential in this case, otherwise everyone just gets in one another's way. At the very most basic level, the soldier has a chance to pick his shots and make the most of his opportunity. He can attack from the flank or rear where the opponent cannot see him coming and thus will be unable to defend effectively.

If a striking attack is used then it should be decisive, for example, a big kick or strike that will disable or at least severely impair the target. There is no point in being cautious against an opponent who cannot respond. Alternatively, a takedown or hold might be used. This is especially useful in the case where an ally is under serious pressure – getting the opponent off him can be vital to keeping him in the fight.

Fighting a Group

The soldier moves away from one opponent, preventing him attacking (A), while another is both temporarily disabled and forced into a comrade with an eye strike (B). This gives an opportunity to attack the first opponent with a powerful groin kick (C) before returning to push the other two together (D). While they are entangled the soldier strikes them both (E, F and G) and then shuttles back to the single opponent to finish him with another kick (H).

A rear choke is an ideal attack because it not only gains immediate control over the opponent and can be used to pull him away from his intended victim but it also allows the soldier to kill or render the opponent unconscious. However, if the target is moving around a lot, it may not be possible to manoeuvre into the right position for a choke. Options include a simple grab around one arm and the head, pulling the opponent back so that the soldier's comrade gains a free shot.

Alternatively, a rear takedown can be used. The simplest way to do this is to grab the opponent from behind by the shoulders and pull back and down whilst kicking one of his legs away. The kick is a down-and-forwards stomp into the calf, just below the knee. This buckles the knee and drops the opponent to the ground where he can be finished off with the boots.

Work as a Gang

When fighting as part of a group, it is most effective to gang up on individuals and take them out quickly, rather than distributing force equally among the enemy. However, this does mean that the rest of the hostiles must be kept occupied. The same tactics can be used as when a lone fighter faces multiple assailants, along with constant movement and switching between targets. For example, a soldier might make an aggressive movement towards one opponent, perhaps accompanied by a lot of noise suggesting an all-out attack. As the target takes a defensive stance or moves back, the

Quick and Dirty Takedown

Moving to assist a comrade who is under heavy attack, the soldier grabs his target by the face, getting his fingers into the eyes, and drags his head back. A kick to the rear of the leg sends him to the ground. This will not keep him out of the fight for long, but it gains time for the soldier to do something else, such as a finishing stomp or find another target.

soldier then switches target and kicks the hostile fighting his comrade. He then switches back to his first target while his ally exploits his new-found advantage. By helping one another out like this, a group of trained fighters can quickly overwhelm a force of determined but less skilled opponents who fight as individuals.

Distracting or confusing an opponent can act as a 'force multiplier', making the soldier more effective. There is no room in all-out combat for subtle feints and misdirection; the opponent will probably not even notice the sort of feint that a trained boxer or mixed martial artist would pick up on. Thus misdirection must be tailored to the opponent; the secret is to either show him something that he absolutely must react to, or to exploit his instinctive responses.

Going in Hard

One way to do this is to initiate a big, graphic attack, e.g. by stepping into kicking range and starting to bring a foot up to chamber a kick. If the opponent fails to react, the kick is certain to succeed and can be launched with confidence. To avoid being soundly booted the target must react, perhaps by aborting whatever he was about to do and sidestepping

. . . .

The most effective attacks catch an enemy by surprise, or are launched after he has been placed in a defensive mind-set. An enemy who does not know what is happening cannot react effectively, and one who is trying not to lose will be defeated by a force that is fighting to win. Psychological tactics are used to create the most productive environment for physical actions.

10

If an enemy can be demoralized or distracted so that he cannot fight effectively, the battle becomes much easier. The opposition might even give up without a fight.

Distraction, Misdirection & Psychological Techniques

Going in Hard

There is no room for half measures in combat. Every blow must be delivered for maximum effect, giving the opponent no chance to collect his wits and start fighting back.

or moving back. At the least, his guard will come down to try to fend off the kick. This enables the soldier to put his foot back down, stepping closer as he does, and launch a strike to the head that will go over the opponent's lowered guard.

A barrage of straight strikes will cause the target to move his guard to cover the frontal line, at which point hooked strikes will have a clear path. Switching from straight to hooked shots and from head to body blows, as well as mixing in kicks and knees, will defeat an opponent who has 'gone defensive'. The first blows are not feints as such; they are entirely real. They may not have all that much effect but they serve the purpose of pulling the opponent's defence onto a given line of attack and thus opening others.

An opponent who is obviously on the defensive is less of a threat than one who is attacking. Thus the soldier will wherever possible try to force his opponent into a defensive mind-set. If he can do this then he can pick his shots more carefully than if he was trying to slip them through the gaps in an opponent's attack.

On the Front Foot

Driving the opponent onto the defensive can require little more than an aggressive and confident demeanour. Noise helps; loud noises are one of the instinctive fears that all humans have. Thus screaming in an opponent's face may make him flinch and abort his intended attack. He will probably cover his head if startled in this way – this is an instinctive reaction and is hard for the conscious mind to overrule. A big shout and obviously chambered fist aimed at the face may cause the opponent to cover his head, leaving himself wide open to a massive kick to the groin.

This sort of gross and blatant deception may seem unworkable to

SWAT Tip: Barrage of Noise

SWAT entry teams make a lot of noise as they enter a hostile building, shouting out commands to surrender and identifying themselves as heavily armed law enforcement personnel. This helps avoid mistakes, such as an innocent person trying to resist what looks like an attack, but just as importantly it disorientates and intimidates the targets. Distraction of this nature can make all the difference.

Aggression

Aggressive body language, threats and shouting can be extremely intimidating and can cause an opponent to 'fold up' before any physical attacks have been made. Effective fighters must be able to both use and resist such tactics.

Surprise Attack

Building-entry teams are extremely vulnerable as they make their initial moves. To compensate they use distraction and surprise, and attack from unexpected directions. The same principles apply to personal combat; it's the one you don't see coming that takes you down.

those more used to the subtleties of sport martial arts, but it works in all-out combat. Noise and aggression are also profoundly important psychological tools. Many fights are 'won in the opponent's mind', i.e. by causing a failure of his will to fight. Someone who has been hit and in pain may well decide to give some back, but if he is faced with an opponent who seems confident and unstoppable then his anger may well be overwhelmed by his fear.

This is especially important when facing a group. If the soldier can take out one of the hostiles (ideally a leader) quickly and graphically then the others may decide to disengage. This is not guaranteed, of course, but it is possible for one man to put a group on the defensive and then scatter them. Had they held their nerve and attacked cooperatively, his chances would have been poor.

Thus it is possible to even or stack the odds by good use of combat psychology. Fortunately, this coincides with good tactics – confident and aggressive attacks work on both the physical and psychological levels; hurting the opponent wears down his body and his will.

Distractions and Tricks
Other distractions and related tricks are possible. Throwing something in an opponent's face will usually make him flinch. This is a poor idea if he is

holding a gun as he will probably pull the trigger by reflex. But for an unarmed attacker or one armed with a blade or blunt instrument, the flinch can be useful. It will not last long, however, and it will be almost certainly followed by a vigorous attack. So a distraction of this sort must be exploited immediately and ruthlessly.

Disguising intent is useful in most circumstances and vital when facing weapons. If the opponent realizes that the soldier is about to act, he will probably fail. On the other hand, if his movement comes as a surprise then he has a distinct advantage. Complete surprise is hard to achieve, and is only likely when the soldier sneaks up on his target, attacks from ambush or blindsides a hostile who is distracted by or engaging a comrade.

It is still possible to surprise someone who is looking right at the soldier if he is not expecting an attack at that precise moment. Even if he fully expects to be attacked, the actual moment of launch can be concealed, which will give the soldier a slight advantage.

One way to conceal intentions is to be constantly moving. The human eye is excellent at spotting something that starts to move from stationary, but is slower to recognize a change in the movement of an object already in motion. Even just a slight movement of the arms, such as some nervous movements of hands raised in surrender, can disguise the critical moment when they begin to move towards the opponent or his weapon.

Keep on Moving

It is extremely easy to spot an attack beginning if it is made by someone who stands still and then throws his punch or kick. If he is moving around, opening and closing distance and circling his opponent, then any given step looks like any other; recognition of the attack may take place a little later; too late to defend perhaps. Movement also creates ambiguity; it is hard to read the precise distance to someone who is moving. This creates doubt as to whether either combatant is within range to strike or be struck.

Just as importantly, there is a tendency to gather yourself before attacking, which is extremely obvious if you are standing still. Someone who sees his opponent crouch slightly, take a deep breath and hunch his shoulders cannot fail to

realize that an attack is imminent. Movement both reduces this tendency and makes any 'tells' that do happen far less obvious.

Making a Noise

Intent can also be concealed by verbal means. Nobody expects to be attacked while they or the opponent are in mid-sentence, and telling an opponent that you will comply with his commands can be surprisingly effective. Thus the soldier might raise his hands, saying 'okay, you got me' or something similarly innocuous. Even if the would-be captor does not speak the same tongue, body language, tone and inflection will all give the impression of submission. The onslaught that occurs a second later should then be a surprise.

Another deception measure that is sometimes applied is to react excessively to any hold that an opponent has taken. This is mainly used when trying to escape from a come-along or restraint; it will not

SWAT Tip: Special Forces Tip: Sudden Beats Fast

Some people move faster than others, but often what counts is catching the opponent by surprise. A movement that begins unexpectedly is more likely to succeed than one that is blindly fast but preceded by some kind of warning. Sudden and fast is the way to go, of course.

work against someone who wants to choke the soldier to death. By squirming and making a lot of noise, the soldier gives the impression that he is in worse pain than he is actually suffering. The captor is not likely to loosen a grip out of mercy but he may be put off guard by how effective his hold seems to be. Meanwhile, the soldier is in fact not squirming around in pain but beginning to seek a release from the hold.

Hunter is Hunted

The use of the predator/prey switch is another useful gambit. Humans occupy a position in the food chain where they prey on some creatures and are prey for others. This situation has been artificially altered by tools and weapons, but the instinctive behaviour is still present.

A fighter who thinks he is winning or has a good will to win is in 'predator' mode; even more so if he is facing a submissive opponent who seems to be surrendering. This is classic prey behaviour and reinforces the 'predator' mind-set.

If the 'prey' suddenly launches an aggressive assault, perhaps accompanied by noise, then the predator/prey switch can be triggered. This is the equivalent of a primitive human about to throw his spear at a grazing deer when a sabre-toothed tiger bursts out of the bushes. Suddenly, the primitive man is in prey mode; he must

escape this fearsome predator or be slaughtered and eaten.

The same thing happens at a psychological level when an apparently defeated enemy suddenly becomes a major threat. At least, the would-be captor will be startled and slow to react. At best, he will be plunged into prey mode, fighting to

On the Front Foot

Take hold of the weapon arm as you grab the head (A), pulling the latter up and back (B). This exposes the throat for an edge-of-hand strike (C). Take the opponent down and choke him before he can recover from the blow (D).

survive instead of to win. He may be half-hearted or even give up entirely; it is possible to completely defeat an opponent in his own mind, turning what should have been a hard fight into the simple matter of delivering a beating.

This, perhaps, is the crux of the matter. Someone who is trying to win is likely to defeat an opponent who is trying not to lose. The 'will to win' or 'fighting sprit' is all about maintaining an offensive mind-set geared towards winning. Psychological gambits attack that fighting sprit, forcing the enemy into a defensive mind-set where, perhaps ironically, he is much easier to defeat.

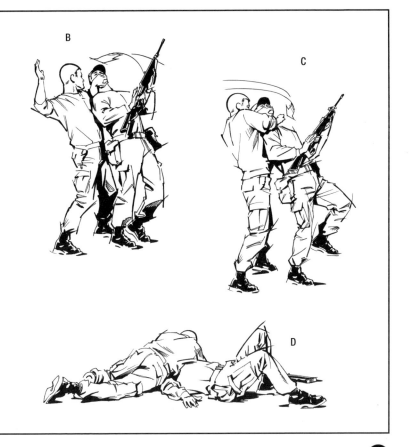

PART THREE: TRAINING

As noted elsewhere, when violence begins then the soldier fights with what he has. If his rifle is not available or has malfunctioned then he must manage without it. If he is out of condition or lacks certain skills then he must somehow make up for this deficiency. Guts and determination can do so much, but it is possible that the soldier may simply be in an impossible situation.

Combat is, to a great extent, a game of odds. Each advantage that the soldier can obtain stacks the odds a little in his favour. Tools and weapons, skills, tactics and physical fitness all add to his overall capabilities. These things are developed during training. Of course, none of them is worth a thing if not driven by a will to win and a desire to fight intelligently but this, too, is developed by good training.

Military and law enforcement personnel have little time to spend on unarmed combat training. This is not their main function, after all. Thus training must be efficient and give a good result for the time invested in it. It is not always possible to measure how highly trained a given soldier is until violence breaks out. At this point, any deficiency becomes glaringly apparent.

A well-trained soldier or police officer will react to a situation almost before it begins, picking up on small 'tells' from a potential aggressor or

opponent that something is about to happen. He will be able to read his opponent's intentions and counter them and, more importantly, he will be able to impose his own will on the fight. Good training goes beyond giving the soldier some skills to use; it makes their use instinctive and efficient. This is absolutely necessary in combat, where there is no time to think carefully about what to do next, and where a mistake can be fatal.

Physical training serves two purposes. Most obviously, it increases the soldier's physical capabilities. His strength and endurance are increased, along with a less readily apparent factor termed conditioning. Conditioning is not exactly the same as fitness; it is more to do with how used the soldier's body is to a given activity. A well-conditioned athlete can perform the same task with less effort than a poorly conditioned one. If they have the same level of fitness then he will be able to last longer – effectively they both have the same size of fuel tank but the well-conditioned athlete's engine is more fuel-efficient for that activity.

Conditioning vs Fitness

Conditioning is specific whereas fitness is often more general. A soldier who works his core muscles a lot will be more efficient in activities using them, e.g. grappling and wrestling, but may not get any real benefit when it comes to a long-distance run. This is why apparently very physically fit people sometimes struggle with a new activity; conditioning must be built for any

. . . .

Fitness and skills training overlap with mental preparation. The habit of finishing an exercise when exhausted translates to an increased will to win in a fight.

11

The adage 'train hard, fight easy' is not really true; fights are always hard. What good training does is stop them being impossible.

Physical Training

given activity. For unarmed combat, the most valuable physical training is the kind that builds relevant conditioning as well as promoting general fitness.

Physical training also has a mental dimension. It is hard work and often painful, and a soldier who is used to confronting these difficulties in training will build a habit of success that carries over into other activities. Fighting on when 'gassed' (exhausted) requires a level of mental toughness that is built over long periods of hard training. Finishing a run with a heavy pack whilst desperately tired contributes to that level of toughness, as does pushing through the pain barrier in any form of physical training.

The main elements of physical training are strength, endurance and flexibility. The latter is not a major concern for those training in military unarmed combat. A certain degree of mobility is necessary to function, but anyone capable of carrying out the duties of a soldier already has that level of flexibility. Soldiers do not train to kick enemies in the head and simply do not need to put in the hours of effort required to achieve that level of capability.

Military training might include some stretching, but for the most part it concentrates on the ability to exert force and to keep on doing it, in other words, it develops strength and endurance. Gym equipment is used, of course, but for the most part military physical training is done on a fairly large scale. Since it is not possible to have enough gym space or equipment for large numbers of personnel, the primary resource is body weight, i.e. soldiers work for much of the time on exercises using only their own bodies.

SWAT Tip: Do It, or Don't Try at All!

A SWAT officer will take a shot or use an unarmed technique because he is confident it will work. He will not make a hopeful attempt at something he is not sure about, because that will probably make things worse.

Running

Running is an excellent general fitness builder, and develops mental strength as well. While any reasonably flat area can be used for runs, there are ways to get more out of the exercise. One is to run carrying heavy kit. This serves the purpose of getting the soldier used to the weight and heft of his gear as well as building endurance at performing arduous tasks whilst carrying it.

Realistic Preparation

Troops in a combat zone have to carry their weapons and equipment everywhere they go. It is thus necessary to train while encumbered with this equipment. A firefight is not the place to find out that you cannot run or fight in full gear.

Another variation on the running theme is hill sprinting. Running uphill is extremely hard work, especially while carrying a load. This can be done as a team-building exercise, with runners racing up the hill in relays or as pairs with soldiers taking it in turns to carry each other on their backs.

Another alternative, often used indoors where space is limited, is shuttle runs or 'wind sprints', whereby the soldier jogs the length of a hall then turns and sprints back, using a powerful push-off on the turn to get quickly up to speed. Sprinting both ways is an alternative, but the cycle of jog/sprint/jog/sprint is an effective method for building good recovery, i.e. the speed at which the body recovers from a burst of intense activity whilst doing something less arduous but still demanding.

Push-Ups and Related Exercises

Push-ups (or press-ups) seem to be the mainstay of military activity to some soldiers, notably those going through basic training. They build upper body strength, which is essential for anyone hoping to function whilst wearing heavy equipment. There are numerous variations on the theme, some of which are more useful than others.

Quick, short dips might create the impression of intense activity but a slower and deeper push-up works

Push-Ups: Building Core Strength

There are many variations on the common push-up, and these can serve to show how unfamiliar activity is much harder than something the soldier is conditioned to. Something as simple as altering hand position makes push-ups vastly more difficult, at least until the soldier's body gets used to the new activity.

the muscles harder. Hand position can be varied from very close to the body to very wide apart, and holding the 'down' position for a second or two each time makes the whole exercise more taxing. A lower number of reps (repetitions) done like this will produce an equal amount of benefit and effort.

As well as grinding out endless 'straight' push-ups, it is possible to incorporate them into other exercises. Squat-thrusts are performed by holding the push-up position and hopping both feet at once as close to the body as possible then extending back out. Or, the feet can be alternated; one leg extended and one close in, swapping their positions on each rep.

Treadmill exercises are similar, but the soldier does not put his feet down close to his body. Instead, he bends each leg and brings it up close to the body and holds it off the ground with the other extended and grounded for support. The position is constantly switched in a series of fast 'horizontal running' movements.

Push-ups are also a component of the infamous 'burpee', which is also known by a variety of other names. The exercise starts in a squat position, from which the soldier kicks his feet out backwards and lands in an extended push-up position, absorbing the impact by performing the 'down' half of a push-up. He immediately drives down hard with

Free Weights

There are some excellent multigyms and fitness machines available, but free weights have additional advantages. As well as lifting the weights, the soldier has to balance and control them. This increases the effort required and prevents the exercise becoming too specific.

the arms, springing back up and bringing the feet back up to land in a squat. From here the soldier springs straight up in the air, and upon landing drops straight down into the squat again, from which position the whole process is repeated.

Abdominal Crunches

The core muscles of the body are extremely important for most military activities, especially unarmed combat. A weak core manifests itself in a posture that is readily broken by an opponent, leading to the soldier being taken down or dragged around and unable to fight back effectively. Lifting, carrying and grappling with someone are all dependent on a good core, so a training programme will normally include exercises to develop these muscles.

Slow abdominal crunches are better than fast, jerky ones. They should be performed with the legs bent, and the soldier should not drag himself up by the head. Instead he should lift from the abdominal muscles. Crunches are often performed with both feet on the floor (the legs should be bent, not straight) but a slightly different set of muscles can be targeted by bringing one knee up on each rep and twisting the torso slightly towards it.

As a variation, the soldier can lie back and only lift his shoulders a little way off the ground, using his abdominal muscles to bring one or

Abdominal Crunches

The core muscles are used in almost all movements and activities a human body can carry out. A 'six-pack' might look good, but more importantly a highly toned set of abs supports everything else. It is worth varying the type of crunches performed to ensure that all the abdominal muscles are targeted.

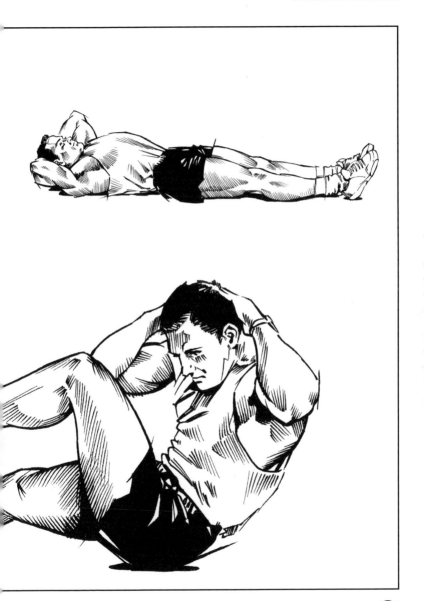

Slow Crunches

Slamming out hard, fast crunches might look impressive, but the best effect is obtained by performing the movement slowly. Releasing the crunch should also be done slowly; flopping limply back to the ground wastes half the exercise.

both legs up towards him. His aim is to get his knee and head as close together as possible pulling both towards each other. Alternatively, the legs can be kept raised and drawn up by bending the knee, either one at a time or both at once.

Squats and Lunges

Squats and lunges work the leg muscles and the core of the body by bending the legs under load. The exercise can be augmented by adding weights, either held in the hands or on a bar across the shoulders. A heavy pack makes squats particularly arduous as the soldier must apply extra effort to balance the pack's weight.

A squat is performed from a standing position by bending the legs as close to right angles as possible (but not beyond) and holding the position for a short period before returning to the squat position. The arms can be held out forwards for balance. This exercise places the quadriceps (thigh muscles) under great strain and increases their endurance, but can strain the knees if the squat is too deep.

An alternative is to squat and kick. The soldier drops into a squat and launches a front kick using alternate legs each time he straightens up. The effort of getting back upright is focused on one leg at a time, while the other uses a different set of muscles for the kick. Further difficulty

is added by the necessity of maintaining balance.

Lunges are much like a fore-and-back squat. The soldier's feet are set apart to front and rear rather than being below his shoulders. The back leg bends as if trying to lower the knee to the floor while the lead leg bends to permit the whole body to be lowered. The torso remains upright throughout. One way to do this exercise is to make repeated lunges and then to swap the foot positions over. Alternatively, the soldier can jump up slightly as he returns to the upright position and swap his feet in the air. It us also possible to 'walk' in this position, stepping though in the high position and then lowering into the next lunge before repeating the process.

Striking Equipment

Hitting a heavy bag, kick shield or focus pads can provide an excellent workout. It is easy to fall into a rhythm of mindlessly banging away at the pads or bag, but while this does have some benefits, if used efficiently, much more can be gained from this kind of workout because these drills can be used to build skill at the same time as fitness.

The most basic use of striking equipment is to learn and develop the striking tools that a soldier will need. Initially any given technique is practiced in isolation so that it can be perfected. It is then added into

Squats and Lunges

Both squats and lunges work the muscles of the legs, but care must be taken not to allow the front knee to bend past 90 degrees. The joint is weak in this position and may suffer damage under a heavy load such as a deep squat or lunge.

combinations and sequences of techniques, which include some movement. When working with the heavy bag the options are limited because the bag does not move around all that much, but it is still possible to train realistically.

For example, the classic combination of lead/cross/ roundhouse kick seems straightforward until it is attempted for real. It can be surprisingly difficult to get the range right to deliver maximum power from each shot, and to learn to set up the next shot whilst delivering the current one. The soldier can get more from the drill by incorporating movement, e.g. starting out of range each time and moving aggressively forwards to deliver the first shot, then stepping away diagonally to the side after the kick.

Pad Work

Working with striking equipment is effective both for building skills and developing fitness. When learning a technique for the first time, the emphasis should be on skills alone. Later it can be drilled with an intensity that rivals any other form of workout.

Heavy Bag

The heavy bag can also be used in ways that are not immediately obvious. The soldier can practice striking from the clinch with a bag, by closing in to deliver a series of blows then clinching the bag with one arm and employing knees and close-range strikes. It takes some time before good, powerful shots can be delivered at extreme close quarters so this is the time to learn – rather than in the middle of a brawl.

The clinch and break can be used as part of a drill, for example, covering up and crashing in to clinch the bag, delivering a couple of close strikes, then pushing it vigorously away and launching longer strikes as if exploding out of a clinch. This is really the only time when the bag should be swinging about – a good strike does not push the bag, it dents it and makes it shudder.

Kick Shields

Kick shields are (obviously) primarily useful in developing the power and technique of kicking and kneeing techniques. They can be used to learn both the actual kick and the set-up required for it. The simplest version of this is learning to get the distance right for any given kick, and perfecting the footwork required to move into the attack. As an alternative, it is possible to practice a defensive kick by having the shield-holder advance. If the kick is launched too soon it will fall short or be very weak; too late and it will not develop properly and will be smothered by the pad.

Kick shields can be used to practice combinations of kicks. For example, the soldier can step in with a front kick, driving the shield-holder back a step, then launch a roundhouse kick as a follow-up as the shield-holder turns to present the shield to this new angle of attack. Kicking drills can be made competitive to get more out of them. For example, the challenge might be to drive the shield-holder back so many steps in as few kicks as possible. This is mainly useful with push kicks, but similar competitive drills can be used with other techniques.

Kick shields can also be used for endurance drills, for example, a challenge to deliver as many 'good' kicks as possible in a set time. A good kick might be defined as one that deeply dents the shield or feels solid to the shield-holder. The shield-holder can count out loud as the good ones land; if he says nothing then everyone knows that was a poor kick that just landed. The kicker's pride and competitive spirit will ensure that the next one will be better.

Knee strikes and other attacks can also be trained for with kick shields. A barrage of strikes can be thrown, with the same sort of challenge as above. This encourages tired soldiers to keep hitting hard and also reinforces a critical point about unarmed combat – it is all very well to hit fast, but not to the point where strikes become weak and ineffectual. Hard is better than fast, though hard and fast is the way to go.

Heavy Bag

It is not possible to unload powerful techniques like front kicks into a small, hand-held pad. This means a heavy bag is essential for training these techniques. It not only provides resistance but also builds confidence in the technique; feeling the impact and seeing the result will convince the soldier that his kick is an effective weapon in a way that no amount of verbal reassurance can match.

Focus Pads

Focus pads are the most flexible of all striking equipment. It is not possible to take full-power kicks on a focus pad, but hand and elbow shots can be put in hard. Focus pads can be used for fairly passive drills where the soldier just bangs in a few shots, or for set-pieces, such as the aforementioned lead/cross/ roundhouse kick. In this case the pad-man drops the pad to his thigh, facing outward, and the power of the kick is kept at a tolerable level.

More demanding pad drills can be constructed. For example, the pad-man can move around and 'flash' targets by keeping the pads 'closed', i.e. facing towards himself. When the soldier sees a pad face he must hit it with some appropriate strike – and he must do so hard and fast before the pad 'closes' again. This teaches the soldier to maintain a vigilant readiness to launch a strike or kick at any target that presents itself. This drill can be fairly static or highly mobile, with the pad-man leading the movement.

Focus pads can also be used to keep the soldier on his toes. A swipe at head height represents a hook punch; thrusting the pad straight out is a straight punch. As a result, a soldier whose guard has a tendency to become sloppy or who is not maintaining good balance will soon correct himself after taking a few light blows.

This sort of pad work can be extremely demanding. The soldier must be constantly on the move, guard up, ready to attack or defend, and must be able to deliver a good solid strike to whatever target he is presented with.

Perhaps the hardest part of this is remaining alert throughout, but being 'on the ball' even when very tired makes for highly effective fighters.

Focus pads are not just used for strike or strike-and-kick drills. They can be used for fitness work, e.g. the pad-man takes a mount position and presents the pads. The soldier must then deliver a series of upwards strikes. After a set number, perhaps six, good strikes have been landed the pad-man begins to drop hooking shots with the pads, aiming at the soldier's head. The soldier covers up and rides the strikes, seeking to catch an arm and pull the pad-man down. From there he gets a five-second breather, then must release and the cycle begins again.

A variety of similar drills can be used, and the focus pads can be used as part of a takedown drill. For example, the pad-man comes in swinging and the soldier jams his strikes, taking a head clinch. The pad-man presents the pads for an upwards knee strike, then the soldier uses a rotation takedown. The pad-man lands on his back and again presents the pads for the soldier to drop shots into.

Striking Post

Martial arts striking posts can be used to train a range of blows including punches and hammerfists. The latter use the base of the hand and not the knuckles.

Focus Pad Drills

Focus pads are extremely versatile training tools. They can be used for knee and elbow strikes as well as punches. Kicks can also be trained, but not at full power. The pads can also be used in unusual or awkward situations, such as striking from the ground or at a downed opponent. The pad-man can also use the pads to strike with, forcing the soldier to flow between attack and defence when necessary.

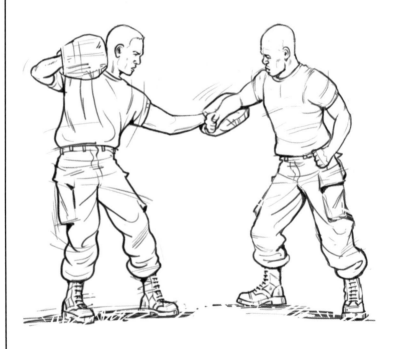

It is all very well to have good skills and the fitness to back them up, but unless those skills can be applied amid the chaos of a fight they are worthless. 'Application' activities, such as sparring, serve more than one purpose, of course. They are physically demanding and painful, which builds fighting spirit and fitness at the same time. They are also somewhat competitive, which helps draw out that indefinable 'will to win' and causes everyone involved to raise their game to match one another. First and foremost, however, application work is all about teaching the soldier to keep his head under combat conditions and to intelligently apply what he has learned.

Too much application work is counterproductive. Bad habits are reinforced rather than good ones, and injuries are inevitable. It is better to train in a pyramid style, with skills and fitness work as the foundations and application as the apex. Each round of application work produces new lessons, which are then incorporated in training. Bad habits are ironed out and new skills developed to cover weaknesses.

. . . .

The time to make mistakes is in training, not in combat. Nothing works exactly as planned, and an important part of application work is learning to cope with a variety of situations.

12

Application work is all about trying out skills in relative safety while there is still time to learn from mistakes.

Application Work

Sparring and Milling

Sparring
Sparring is an important component of training with striking skills. It can be used in many forms and for slightly different purposes. The most basic form looks a lot like boxing, with fighters restricted to boxing-type rules – hand strikes only, no grappling and so forth. The level of contact can be varied depending on whether the session is geared towards technical development or pressure-testing of skills and mind-set. Heavy sparring is most common; lighter, more technical sparring is mainly used to develop skills for sporting contests.

Special Forces Tip: Use What You Have!

Special forces soldiers do not try to invent new capabilities mid-mission. Their plan plays to their strengths and abilities. They will not attempt something they do not know how to do; instead they will find a way to apply the skills they do have.

Likewise, kickboxing-type sparring, which by definition includes kicks, is rarely used. The kicking skills used by military personnel are somewhat basic; it requires rather more skill to use a kick in a sparring context and not hurt the opponent too much than to simply hoof him. Thus sparring with kicks is too likely to cause injury to be commonly used as a military training aid. The same goes for knees and elbows and, of course, the strikes that are intended to be lethal. Thus sparring is somewhat artificial, although it does have benefits in terms of fitness, learning to read the opponent's intentions, timing and distance and, crucially, dealing with the adrenaline and fear associated with fighting someone.

Milling
Milling is a variation on the sparring theme. Defence is discouraged; soldiers are expected to pile into one another and keep hitting. This improves conditioning and builds an aggressive mind-set. It is also closer to a real fight, in that a soldier will not 'box' his opponent, slipping punches and wearing him down, in a war zone. He will want to steamroller whoever is in front of him and move on. Milling is all about that level of aggression and teaches an important lesson – if you don't like getting hit, then you should be hitting the opponent to stop him doing it.

The chief difference between

Special Forces Tip: Stay Flexible

It is vital to remain flexible and not fixate on a single goal. A fighter who plans to throw a lead/cross/kick combination, and whose opponent stumbles sideways when the cross hits him, must change his plan rather than trying to launch a kick he is out of position for.

milling and sparring is that sparring is a two-way street. There is some accepted give-and-take; the soldier spars with his partner and both develop their skills. Milling is different; it is one soldier against another. Cooperative give and take will result in getting hurt, so each soldier tries to give more than he takes. Milling is good fight training not because it develops skills – it is usually more violent than skillful – but because it puts the soldier in a fight situation and gets him used to dealing with violence in an environment where failure will not be fatal. Mistakes made in milling are painful but the lessons learned can save lives.

Rolling and Grappling Drills

The term 'rolling' is used by sport martial artists to describe a (relatively) friendly grappling match. It is thus the equivalent of sparring in many ways. The participants might start standing

up and look for a takedown, or on their knees in which case there are usually rules against standing up. Either way, the aim is to pin the opponent or apply a submission hold that forces him to 'tap out', i.e. to submit by tapping his opponent or the floor.

Rolling

Rolling does develop grappling skills to a high degree, but the benefits of this may not be immediately apparent. Military training discourages soldiers from going to the ground at all, and certainly does not advocate rolling around for several minutes looking for a choke or arm bar. However, rolling has some very significant benefits. It is a tremendous whole-body workout and builds mental toughness. The desire not to lose inspires soldiers to tolerate discomfort from a not-quite-good-enough submission hold while they seek a release.

Rolling teaches soldiers to keep calm and think clinically in combat.

Constant utmost effort will work in milling, but in a grappling situation it is a guarantee that the soldier will 'gas' (become exhausted) very quickly and be defeated. He must instead learn to pick his moment and make a maximum effort when it will do most good.

Grappling

Grappling is far less likely to result in injuries than milling or sparring, despite the fact that the techniques applied are dangerous. Soldiers learn how to put a choke or joint lock on hard and fast but with sufficient control that it does no harm unless they want it to. In the field the same skills would be used to lock in the technique quickly and efficiently, and to prevent the subject escaping from it.

In addition to other benefits, competitive grappling of this sort also builds team spirit. Wrestling has been a part of the 'warrior' ethos for all of recorded time, and it still serves a useful purpose today. It is an intensely physical activity that can also be good fun. Successfully submitting to one another builds soldiers' confidence in one another and in their own capabilities.

'Bulling' is often used as a warm-up exercise for grappling. Both partners start standing up with a typical wrestling grip in place – right and around the back of the partner's neck and left hand in the crook of his arm. From here, the partners pull and push one another around, learning to feel what each other is starting to do and either counter it or use the momentum to gain an advantage. Bulling can be done lightly, in order to develop a sensitivity to the opponent's intentions, or harder, as a workout. There should be no takedowns though; this is a limited exercise with a specific purpose in mind.

'Fighting for Grips'

'Fighting for Grips' is another useful exercise. It can be done competitively, with both partners simultaneously trying to obtain a useable grip, which would lead to a takedown, or the partners can take it in turns to play the role of the attacker and the defender.

Variations on this theme include 'swimming for underhooks', whereby the attacking partner tries to obtain a double underhook position (with both arms around the opponent's body under his arms) and the defender trying to stop him. A movement somewhat like swimming is used to force the arm down between the opponent's arm and body. A similar drill can be used when trying to obtain a head clinch.

On the ground, 'positional rolling' can be used for the same purpose. This can be a set-piece drill where one partner proceeds through a series of transitions to different positions with no resistance or it can be competitive, with both partners trying to achieve a dominant position and to reverse the other's advantage. All of these drills are extremely hard work and teach soldiers to obtain a

Takedown Applications

While it is unlikely that firearms would be brought into a grappling session, the same skills used to take down and choke an unarmed opponent can be used to silently tackle an enemy sentry. The confidence necessary to attempt this must be built in training.

Fighting for Grips

One of the most important parts of combat grappling is establishing a good grip on the opponent. One way to practice is to use competitive drills, with both fighters trying for a head clinch, underhooks or any other solid grip.

Throws and Takedowns

In combat there is only one chance to succeed with a throw or takedown. Endless practice lets the soldier instinctively position himself correctly and follow through with the right mechanics for a powerful throw.

dominant position quickly and efficiently. Fumbling about in the middle of a fight leads to defeat; well-practiced skills are essential.

Dirty Sparring

Dirty sparring can be done at medium intensity or full-contact. Either way it is a tough mental challenge as well as being physically demanding. The training area is often very restricted, with both participants required to remain in a small area (e.g. 2m by 2m [6.5ft by 6.5ft]) to force them to fight at close quarters rather than 'boxing' each other. Strikes are permitted only with the gloves, to prevent injuries, and takedowns are not allowed. However, the participants are permitted to clinch and to strike from the clinch.

There are two basic strategies in this drill. One is to treat it like milling and just keep on throwing big shots, but inevitably something will come the other way.

The other alternative is to close in and clinch. What then happens is both fighters struggle to control each other's striking arms and to land shots of their own. The effort of pulling an arm out of a clinch and landing one or more telling shots before the soldier is tied up again is immense, but if the bout degenerates into a static clinch then the fighters will be separated. This opens up the range a little and allows a new onslaught of big shots.

This drill has benefits similar to milling, teaching soldiers to take advantage of any weakness the opponent may have, but it also teaches them to fight smart and sneaky. The trick is to be able to limit what the opponent can do whilst getting a few blows in. There is no retreat, so the soldier must fight where he stands and do well or take a beating.

A variant on this drill uses two-minute rounds, which each participant staying on for two in a staggered rotation. So each soldier has one round where he is reasonably fresh and one when he is exhausted and his opponent is not. His strategy will have to change in the second round, when the bout becomes a matter of survival as much as anything else.

Other Application Drills

A number of other application drills can be used to develop skills or add realism to training. Some are straight 'fighting' exercises; others are more tactical in nature.

'Gloves vs Grappler'

One very useful drill is 'gloves vs grappler'. One partner is given boxing gloves and can only strike. The other is bare-handed and can only grapple. This drill only works if the striker comes forwards and attacks; if he backs off then the drill is pointless. His role is to pressurize

Specialist Applications

Military unarmed combat training teaches a number of specialist applications not used elsewhere. A rear takedown of this sort is unlikely to be useful in a sporting contest, but a soldier who may have to take out a sentry or enemy combatant will find it effective.

Grappler vs Striker

This drill develops fighting spirit as well as specific skills. The grappler must close in despite a barrage of blows and bring his opponent under control. He cannot win by retreating; he must face the attacks and deal with them.

the grappler and hurt him with repeated medium-intensity blows. The grappler must close in to the striker and shut him down. He 'wins' when he ties up the striker so that he cannot effectively land a blow. This might be in a standing position or a takedown may be required. This is not a competitive drill; the striker cannot win. What he can do is keep striking for as long as possible and make the grappler work for his victory.

Rolling can be made more realistic by allowing some striking and/or dirty tricks. Maintaining a dominant position becomes more problematical when the opponent tries to push you off by the eyeballs.

Obviously it is not possible to take the 'biting and gouging' aspects of dirty fighting to an extreme in training, but it is worth incorporating them. Apart from anything else, soldiers fight the way they train and if they have trained for a clean, competition-rules situation they might forget about their arsenal of dirty tricks.

Identifying Vulnerabilities

The fighter must also be made aware of the vulnerabilities of certain positions used in competitive grappling. Grabbing testicles is forbidden in competitive martial arts and drills derived from them. Soldiers and police officers attempting to arrest an opponent or defeat him on the ground must be aware of what the subject might do in order to avoid making themselves vulnerable.

Dirty tricks do not invalidate other grappling methods, but they do change the game somewhat. A disadvantaged fighter can rest on his back if he has the opponent under control, but if the opponent is allowed to strike or inflict pain from this position then escaping becomes rather more urgent. This more accurately simulates a real fight.

Groundfighting Drills

Striking in groundfighting drills illustrates the difficulty in delivering power from this position, and enables the soldier to learn how

Special Forces Tip: It's Done That Way For A Reason

The skills taught to soldiers have been proven in combat. They work. If there was a better way, chances are that would be taught instead.

to both attack and defend when entangled with an opponent on the ground. It may or may not be desirable to train with full-contact strikes. Often lighter blows can be used to limit the risk of injury whilst still maintaining a valuable level of realism.

One good drill that teaches soldiers the reality of close combat on the ground is for one partner to start on his back and his opponent to take any dominant position he chooses. The partner on his back must reverse the position and escape from a delineated area while his opponent simply has to keep him down. Alternatively, the soldier on top can be tasked with disengaging while his opponent tries to hold him down from underneath.

This drill is about time. Pressure can be added by having the addition of a third opponent who closes in slowly and delivers some light blows if the soldier has not yet 'won' the exercise. A timer can be used to set a deadline for escape or to make the exercise competitive.

In all cases, it quickly becomes apparent that the use of dirty tricks will secure an escape much more quickly that relying on a 'clean' position game. Digging elbows or knuckles into the opponent, or grinding a bony forearm across his face, will often cause his grip to weaken and permit a much more rapid escape.

Striking Drills

Striking drills can also be made more challenging. 'Interference' drills can be done two ways – defensive and competitive. In both cases the goal is to deliver as many strikes as possible to a focus pad in a set time; say two or three minutes.

The two-man version of this drill is fairly simple; the pad-man holds the focus pad in the same place relative to his body but can fend off the attacker with his other hand. The soldier must get past the obstacle to deliver his blows.

This becomes more of a challenge when a third participant is introduced. In the defensive version of the drill the third man tries to prevent the soldier from striking the pad by dragging him away, grabbing his arms and so forth. The soldier must disentangle himself, push the interfering opponent away and attack the pad for as long as possible before he is grabbed again and has to repeat the whole process.

The competitive version of the drill has both participants trying to strike the focus pad whilst stopping the other from doing so. They will have to push or drag each other out of the way, which makes the whole exercise far harder and more chaotic than simply delivering a few strikes. They must learn not to lose sight of the goal; the intent is to hit the pad, not to become involved in a wrestling match with someone else.

Striking Drills

Rather than just practicing knee strikes, a useful alternative is for the pad-holder to advance using the pads to throw strikes with. The soldier must deal with this attack and establish a good position despite resistance. The pad holder then gives him the pads for a knee-strike finish. If he has failed to establish a solid base then the strike will be weak.

Shuttle Drills

'Shuttle drills' are good for both technique and situational awareness. The soldier begins between two opponents who have focus pads or kick shields, or one of each. He must deliver enough strikes to both sets of targets to be judged to have won. The pad-men will close in slowly once the drill begins, and will only open the distance if given a reason to do so, such as a push or being driven back by a strong kick.

If the soldier simply fixates on one target he will fail; the other will close him down from behind. Thus he must shuttle between the opponents. His opening move might be to push one away, turning to deliver a kick to the other that will drive him back.

The soldier then goes back to the first target and unloads several powerful strikes until the person supervising the drill calls 'Down!' and that target drops out of the exercise. If he cannot convince the observer that he has done enough, he will have to push that opponent away again while he drives the other back.

A more powerful version of this drill adds the command 'Hurt!' from the observer. A pad-man whose targets are being hit steps back upon hearing 'Hurt!' and stays out of the fight until the observer gestures him back in. A verbal command is not used; the soldier does not know how long his attack has bought him and can still lose if he fixates for too long on the other opponent.

In order to win the soldier must use pushes and blows that drive back one opponent or hurt him enough to keep him out of the fight for a moment, then quickly deliver fight-winning strikes to the other. The drill requires a combination of situational awareness, good tactics and the ability to hit hard.

'Shark Tank' Drill

The 'Shark Tank' is about mental toughness and will to win. Also called a 'gauntlet', the set-up involves several opponents with various pieces of equipment spaced across the drill area. The soldier enters at one end and at each station must use a different combat skill. Each station might be timed, say 30 seconds at each, or a goal might be set at each.

There are many variations on this drill. The following six-station drill uses goals rather than time. Where a given number of strikes must be delivered, only 'good ones' are counted by the pad-man.

A strike that is ineffectual is not counted; the soldier can only move on when he hears the pad-man shout out the correct number. This ensures maximum effort even when tired – a vital habit to cultivate. The alternative, a set number of seconds delivering blows, is less effective because it permits a tired soldier to hold back on some of the stations.

The shark tank is a test of physical fitness but more importantly, mental toughness and the ability to endure punishment. It is extremely difficult to keep delivering good shots on the back half of the course, but it is there that character is built. Those who falter when it gets tough risk being defeated in a real fight.

Example Shark Tank

Stations can be close together or widely spaced. Either way the soldier must run between them.

Station 1: Straight Shots

The soldier must deliver six solid shots to a focus pad held by a comrade who shouts out the number as each good shot lands, and says nothing if a shot is weak. On hearing 'Six!' the soldier begins his run to the next station.

Station 2: Roundhouse Kicks

The soldier must deliver six good roundhouse kicks to a kick shield held by a comrade, moving on only at the call of 'Six!'

Station 3: Clinches

The soldier faces a comrade wearing boxing gloves, who closes in and launches swinging punches at his head. The soldier must close in and clinch the opponent up so that he cannot strike. Each time he does so, the opponent calls the number. Upon hearing the shout 'Three!' the soldier moves on.

Station 4: Hooks

The soldier must deliver solid hooking strikes to a pad, moving on only when he has landed six.

Station 5: Knee Strikes

The soldier faces a comrade with a kick shield. He must establish a head clinch and deliver six solid knee strikes.

Station 6: Escape

The soldier faces an opponent whose task is to prevent him escaping the drill area. The opponent establishes a wrestling grip or clinch, and the soldier must fight until he escapes.

Shark tanks can be made harder or easier by varying the number of techniques at each station or changing the number of stations. The order can also be important; adding a grappling challenge at the start can be debilitating.

For example, if the drill started with the soldier held down so that he had to first escape from that situation before fighting his way through the gauntlet, his stamina would be drained before he even began.

275

Shark Tank Drill

A shark tank drill simulates an epic battle that goes on far longer than most incidents of unarmed combat. By the time the soldier gets to the end he will be tired and short of breath, making the final grappling match a hard fight indeed.

Station 1

START

Station 2

Station 3

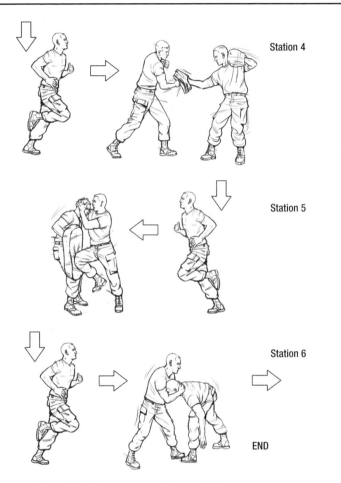

Station 4

Station 5

Station 6

END

**By timing each soldier's progress through the
shark tank, an element of competition is created
that can help get the most out of each run
through the drill.**

Real combat takes place in a fast and fluid environment. The level of violence is shocking and can cause combatants to freeze or panic. This tendency must be overcome in training to ensure that the soldier or police officer can act decisively and effectively even while surprised or confused.

Simple Moves, Controlled Aggression

Thus what works in real combat is simple moves done with determination and aggression. Display teams exist to entertain as much as to inform, and thus a large part of what is seen in a military unarmed-combat display is unlikely to be used in a real fight. The skills are real and the techniques are valid, but in a straight fight even the most skilled personnel will tend to leave the flashy and impressive moves in the box and instead rely on material that does not make a very good display but will win a fight – and fast.

There is no room mid-fight for lofty notions such as 'violence solves nothing'. Once violence has started then it can only be met with force. Military and police personnel will

. . . .

Once violence starts, it only stops when the victor says it does. Heavy blows to the head and body, and aggressive grappling techniques, will determine the outcome.

A soldier's willingness to 'get stuck in' and fight to win counts for more than anything else. If he keeps fighting, he may or may not win but if he gives up, he loses for certain.

Final Notes

Special Forces Tip: No Plan Survives Contact with the Enemy

Special forces units go into action as part of a carefully laid plan, but no mission goes exactly to expectations. The personnel involved must modify their plan to cope with changing circumstances whilst maintaining the overall aim. Losing heart because the plan went awry leads to defeat and possibly death.

usually attempt to resolve a situation without anyone getting hurt; a suspect who surrenders without a fight or an enemy combatant who flees is a victory won at no cost. However, there is a point where only extreme violence will guarantee survival and victory, so personnel must be able to switch rapidly from a 'situation control' mind-set to one of 'fight and win'.

Moral questions, likewise, have no place in a fight. It may occur to a soldier to wonder if the enemy combatants are justified in shooting at him, but the question is rather academic and can be shelved for another time. What matters is that they are shooting, and he needs to deal with what is actually happening. Ambiguous questions about motivation and justification, even if answered, cannot alter the outcome of the situation.

Violence as a Tool

That is not to say that military personnel are encouraged to be bad people by their training. If anything the opposite is true. Very few people ever actually want to hurt someone else, and the military tends to weed out psychopaths who do. Soldiers are trained to use violence when necessary, and to refrain when it is not. They are subject to rules of engagement and tight discipline that makes them less rather than more likely to use their skills when the situation does not warrant it.

The necessity of violence goes with the territory. A soldier or a police officer must understand and accept the concept that he may have to use violence in order to complete his mission or to protect someone. It would be pleasant to live in a world where was never necessary, but we do not and probably never will.

In our unpredictable world, there are plenty of people who want to harm others. Laws, international agreements and earnest attempts to build friendship between different groups can go a long way towards reducing the overall level of conflict in the world but we cannot say for sure if or when violence will break out. The motivations of those who want to want to do harm may vary; often they see themselves as entirely justified.

Hostage Rescue Tip: Shoot/No-Shoot Decision

Hostage-rescue units sometimes cannot be certain who the 'bad guys' and the hostages are. A gunman might be hiding in among non-combatants, and a hostage might make a sudden move that could get him shot. Hostage-rescue personnel must sometimes make a decision to shoot or not based on a fleeting impression of the situation. Good training prepares them for this.

Bodyguard Tip:
Proportionate Response

It is not always possible to act until there is a clear sign than the situation has 'gone hostile', and even then it is necessary to judge the right level of response. Over-eager journalists might have to be pushed away from the client and ten seconds later you may have to deal with an attempt to stab him. Making the right response at the right time is what they pay you for.

This creates a situation where the intended victim has a stark choice between accepting whatever the opposition wants to do to them or fighting back.

When hostiles attack our people, terrorists take hostages or criminals bring violence to the streets where we live, someone has to deal with it. These people operate in a highly dangerous environment and must therefore be trained in skills that will allow them to survive and to defeat the enemy. The same skills can be used by private citizens to defend themselves against attack, and much the same rules apply.

Extreme Threat, Extreme Response

Extreme violence is the only way to deal with an extreme threat, but it must be used judiciously. An argument over a spilt drink or a minor traffic accident is not grounds for using skills that can kill, unless, of course, the other party escalates the issue to the point where an extreme threat does exist. Anyone – police, military or civilian – can unexpectedly be faced with a situation where someone means to seriously hurt or even kill them. If that happens then the aggressor has decided that someone is going to get badly hurt. A trained person has the option to decide who that's going to be.

This is the reality of extreme unarmed combat. A properly trained person not only knows how to cause severe damage to another human being but also when to do it – and when not. Personnel are trained to be responsible and proportionate in their use of force and only when the situation is extreme, such as open combat against armed hostiles, are extreme measures used.

Special Forces Tip: No Suicide Missions

Special forces personnel do not undertake suicide missions. They analyze the situation carefully and find a way to accomplish their task. If it looks to be suicidal, they withdraw and wait for a better opportunity. Choosing when to fight and when to disengage is a vital skill.

The capability for extreme violence must be in place in case this happens, but the soldier or police officer always has the choice of whether or not to use his skills. He will be called upon answer for his actions, as will a civilian acting in self-defence. Any harm done to another person must be justifiable and within the bounds of reasonable conduct.

In short, this means that the techniques shown in this book are intended only for use in an extremely hazardous situation, which cannot otherwise be resolved. Violence is sometimes the only workable option but on any occasion where it is not the only recourse then it is best avoided.

After all, you can't possibly lose a fight that you didn't have.

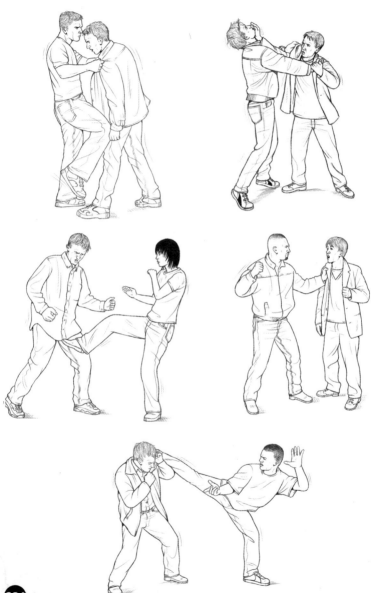

Civilians rarely have to face the extremes of violence that a soldier or police officer might and, in most cases, they have the option to make escape their primary goal. Indeed, police and military personnel responding to a situation will usually have the protection and safety of innocents as a high-priority goal. They face danger so that civilians do not have to.

Unexpected Threats

If a typical civilian goes about their business with due respect for others, and tries not to pointlessly antagonize people, then they are unlikely to be a victim of violence. However, it is possible to be in the wrong place at the wrong time and find you are forced to deal with an extreme situation.

There are three aspects to any threat: physical, legal and emotional. All must be successfully defended against in order to 'win', but the actual means used to defend can vary considerably. Simply getting to the other side of a door, locking it and calling the police is an entirely effective solution to many threatening

. . . .

Stress and fear make simple tasks hard and hard tasks impossible. The simpler a technique, the more likely it is to succeed when it counts.

The simple, straightforward techniques of military unarmed combat are highly effective for civilian self-defence. They can be learned quickly; an advantage for busy people with little time for martial arts training.

Appendices: Civilian Applications

situations. However, sometimes escape is not possible, or may not be acceptable. Escaping physical harm by fleeing is a good option, unless, of course, it means leaving someone else behind to suffer. That might simply not be an option and so the civilian, however outmatched, may decide to stay and fight it out.

It has been well documented that in the case of violent crime, those who suffer harm but fight back (however unsuccessfully) tend to make a better psychological recovery than those who did not resist.

Win-Win, or Win-Lose?

Similarly, defeating an assailant but ending up in jail is not a total 'win', although it may be better than some of the alternatives. This means a civilian must consider the possible consequences of their actions. The law does allow violence to be used in self-defence or in defence of others, but it must be reasonable and proportionate. Soldiers and police officers receive instruction in the use of force that includes both how but also when and why; civilians do not have the benefit of this training unless they have found a good self-defence class.

It is worth stressing the 'good' here. Many martial arts classes claim to teach self-defence, and some do it well. Many, however, miss certain key points or teach rather fanciful applications of their martial art rather than true self-defence techniques. A good class not only teaches simple, workable techniques but also the 'soft skills' of de-escalation and conflict management, and builds an understanding of the relevant law into the training on offer.

Threat Levels

The threats faced by civilians can vary considerably. Some are every bit as extreme as those found in a war zone, and require robust countermeasures. Others are more complex. For example, a potential assailant might use aggressive 'posturing', pushes and grabs to exert dominance without directly causing harm. Deciding what to do about this level of threat is difficult, and many people fear that they will end up in legal trouble if they take any action at all.

The law recognizes that it is necessary to use sufficient force to repel an assault. Assuming that the intended victim did not go looking for trouble, and tried to avoid violence, then if they only did what they genuinely thought they had to, their actions will be legal as self-defence.

Police, military and security personnel are required by their profession to confront threats and deal with them. However, a civilian has several additional options.

The most basic is trying to avoid trouble wherever possible, e.g. by staying away from likely threats such as dark alleys favoured by muggers.

Fight or Flight?

A key tool in self-protection is the willingness to walk away from a confrontation or de-escalate it rather than increasing the tension by insisting on 'winning' or getting the last word in. However, a determined aggressor may decide to keep escalating the situation or even use violence right from the outset. If it becomes obvious that there are no good options remaining, or that non-violent measures are unlikely to work then a private citizen has the right to do whatever is necessary in order to preserve their safety.

The goal in any situation is to end the attack, not necessarily to demolish the opponent. That might be necessary, but the goal of a private citizen is to preserve their safety. If that means making an escape possible, or causing an assailant to decide to back off, then this is just as much a 'win' as leaving him unconscious or unable to fight. A situation that does not become violent thanks to effective use of de-escalation skills ('talking down' an angry or aggressive person) is also a clear victory.

Dealing with a Threat

However, once violence erupts then physical measures are necessary. The intended victim must do what

they need to in order to avoid coming to harm. As a rule, striking techniques are the best option. A person with minimal or no training should avoid getting into a grappling match with an opponent, even if he is equally unskilled.

First Strike

The most basic self-defence tool is to strike the opponent hard in the head. Open hands or hammerfists are the best tools as they will not risk damage to the hand. Knee strikes to the legs and body are also extremely effective. More complex techniques, including most kicks, are not a good option for two reasons.

Many otherwise effective techniques may require more skill than most people possess to use reliably. Perhaps more importantly, civilians are rarely trained to handle the stress of combat, and stress makes people clumsy. An apparently simple task becomes very tricky during mid-fight conditions. Thus, anything complex will probably fail, and a failed technique can leave the user very vulnerable.

Simple is Effective

Thus, for civilians who do not have extensive self-defence training it is best to stick to the simplest of techniques, which mostly means strikes. These are the mainstay of military combat systems for exactly the same reasons that make them

287

Effective Self-Defence Skills

Some martial arts schools claim that fanciful techniques like high kicks are effective self-defence tools. The time wasted on complex, low-percentage nonsense would be much better spent on something more generally useful, such as the 'soft skills' of conflict management, which can de-escalate a situation and prevent violence from happening at all.

Grabs

An attempt to grab is in many ways as serious as a blow. The assailant might only want to drag his victim around and shout at him (which is bad enough) but if he decides to escalate the violence then he is likely to succeed.

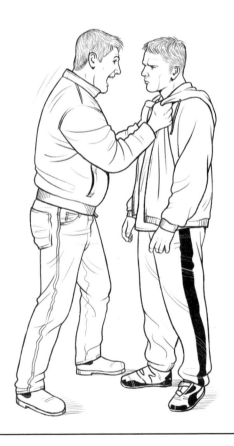

Pushing

Pushing is often used to gauge the victim's response. A passive or frightened reaction may encourage the assailant to escalate the level of violence. Once a situation has 'gone physical', even in a fairly minor way, the intended victim must act decisively or suffer whatever harm the assailant has in mind.

effective civilian self-defence tools. A chin jab, or palm strike to the jaw, is an excellent way to secure release from a clothing grab. In a low-threat situation, for example, where someone is trying to exert dominance or is treading the line between bullying and messing about, it might be possible to twist the grip away and apply a joint lock as a broad hint to desist that will not quite take the situation into the realms of a fight.

If it looks like the aggressor is going to throw a punch, perhaps using the grab to drag the victim onto the blow, then a more violent response is necessary. The chin jab will drive his head back, spoiling any blow he might be intending to throw and also pushing him away from the victim. He may release his grip voluntarily at this point. If not, he has one hand tied up and out of the fight while his intended victim is able to strike with both hands.

First Strike

The straight chin strike can be used as a follow-up after defeating an attempt to grab or strike. There is no point in simply fending off the attack; another one will be immediately launched. However, any time that there is a clear path between hand and head, the opponent can be struck hard enough to put him out of the fight.

Whether the threat is a punch or a grab, it is important to move aside,

Grab and Punch

With a punch on the way, there is no point in fixating on the grab and trying to peel it off or apply a clever wrist lock. The only plus to this situation is that the assailant has tied up one of his hands, and the victim has both free.

out of the path of the incoming arm, and deflect the arm in the opposite direction. If the chin jab is not completely successful in ending the threat, it can be followed up with additional strikes.

The hammerfist another useful close-quarters striking method. It can, of course, be used to demolish an opponent but it is also a good way to break a grab. Nobody picks a fight they think they will lose, so an aggressor is likely to be bigger and stronger than his intended victim. A struggle matching strength against strength probably will not work, but a strike to the head may make him flinch away and let go.

Eye Jabs

While it is an unpleasant concept, an eye strike can be used by anyone to get a result. No amount of bulk or muscle will protect the eyes; they are always vulnerable to a straight strike. There is little real danger of permanently destroying the eyes, but even a marginal blow will cause a flinch. Many people will back off in the face of an opponent who seems willing to attack their eyes; and even if not, then the strike can create an opportunity for a follow-up.

An eye strike requires very little skill, which makes it a good use for the lead hand. It takes long training to become effective at striking with the lead hand; the typical civilian does not possess such skill. The lead hand is

Chin Jab

Release from a one- or two-handed grab can be secured by use of the chin jab. This can be combined with an attempt to dislodge the grab, which has a reasonable chance of success if the attacker's head is driven back. Indeed, he may decide that he wants to let go and retreat.

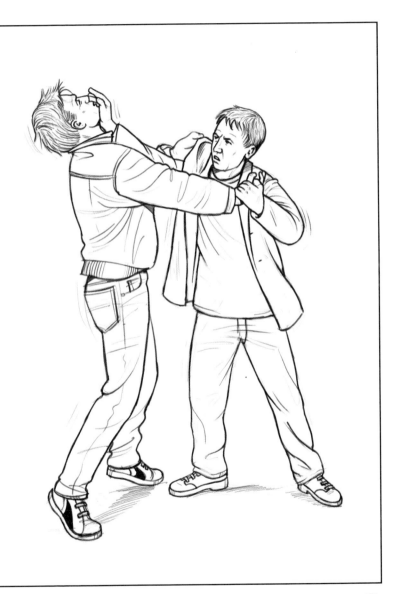

Reading Intentions

The commonest attack thrown in fights, even between supposedly trained people, is the haymaker, or 'big swinging right'. This is usually preceded by a very obvious wind-up, creating an opportunity to duck under it or to launch a more direct attack.

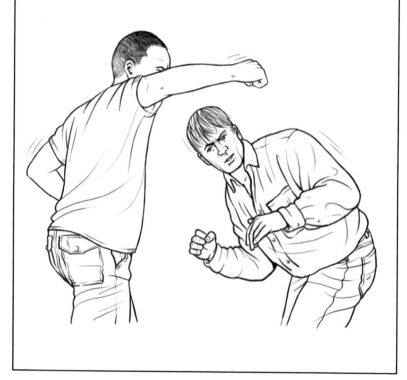

Hammerfist

The hammerfist is an excellent close-quarters striking tool, which requires little room to use. Many people find the hammering movement instinctive, which is an advantage when trying to perform it under stress. Anywhere on the head or face makes a good target.

Eye Jab

The eye jab is a fast movement using the lead hand, and will often literally 'beat the opponent to the punch' if he is winding up to throw a haymaker. Causing him to flinch away from an eye attack is an effective defence; his punch will probably not be thrown and if it is, it will be weak. The strike should travel somewhat upwards into the eyes, taking care not to hit the hard bone of the forehead.

Follow Up

An eye strike will not necessarily put an opponent out of the fight, but it should create an opportunity for a powerful blow. In general, fights are won by whoever lands the first clean, hard shot to the head.

close to the opponent and can land a blow much faster than a strong-hand blow. If the opponent staggers away, an opportunity has been made for escape. If he merely flinches, follow-up blows are necessary.

Groin Strikes

Kicks also have more uses than directly harming an opponent, though this is always useful. For example, a kick to the groin is likely (but by no means certain) to stop an assailant in his tracks. However, it is surprisingly hard to land a clean groin kick, and most attempts do not stop the fight. Indeed, some solid contacts do not stop the fight; much depends on exactly how and where the kick lands, and how determined the assailant is.

Although this does mean that the groin kick is not a perfect solution to all problems, it does tend to make an opponent hesitate. Most people will hunch up or flinch away from a groin strike, or from any blow that seems to be going in that direction. Thus although the kick itself may not stop the fight, it may cause the opponent to hesitate and open him up for something else, especially if it pulls his attention downwards. As his hands drop to protect his groin, his head is open to be hit.

Leg Strikes

Attacking an assailant's legs is a good way to facilitate an escape. A knee to the thigh is unlikely to result in any major injury but it will hurt the opponent a lot, which might be enough to make him want to break off the attack. If not, then it will weaken his leg, making it much harder for him to attack or pursue. Of course, knees can also be used to attack the body or head. It is possible to pull an opponent's head down and finish him with a rising knee strike, but this is unlikely to succeed unless he has been weakened by blows. It is generally better to use straight or roundhouse knee strikes to the body or legs.

A knee strike is an instinctive movement that requires only gross motor control, and does not need great precision. Hitting an opponent almost anywhere will cause pain and damage.

Knee strikes can also be used at very close quarters. These factors make them highly useful for people without much training or who find themselves in a difficult close-quarters fight against a more powerful opponent.

One kick that is potentially useful in civilian self-defence is the sweeping edge-of-foot kick to the shin. This is useful at close quarters, which is where most fights happen. Delivered hard and aggressively, it can inflict sufficient pain to cause an opponent to back off. It will also compromise his balance by pushing his foot away or forcing him to flinch away from the pain.

This can create an opportunity to push the opponent away and escape, or to follow up with additional blows. It may secure release from a grab, because the assailant's attention is directed down to the source of the pain. Any grab will be weakened by broken posture, so kicking a foot away in this manner is likely to be highly effective in escaping from a grab, especially if it is followed up by additional blows or knee strikes.

Other Options

Other measures, such as grappling and takedowns, are unlikely to succeed without some training in their use. If at all possible it is vital to avoid becoming entangled with an opponent, which includes well-meaning attempts to put a restraint on someone. For the civilian who is not trained for conflict and does not have to face violence as part of their job, then the best option is to only fight if it is absolutely necessary and unavoidable.

If an attack does occur despite efforts to avoid trouble, then the goal is to escape from the situation or end it after suffering as little harm as possible. Efforts to intervene in someone else's fight or to restrain a person intent on delivering serious harm, no matter how charitable the intention, usually result in unnecessary injury. Civilians who are attacked should do what they must to end the confrontation, and stay out of any dangerous situation that they do not have to enter.

Groin Strikes

Groin strikes are not an automatic fight-ender. More often than not the strike is fairly marginal, hurting the opponent but not putting him down. It is necessary to be ready to follow up with additional strikes, or to use the opportunity gained to flee.

This philosophy amounts to exactly the same approach that military personnel planning an operation would employ: fight only when it is necessary, and fight as hard as necessary.

Kneeing from the Clinch

Both straight and roundhouse knees can be used from a grappling or 'clinch' situation. Lifting a foot up compromises balance, so it is important to use the opponent to assist. Pulling him onto the strike increases force and prevents loss of balance.

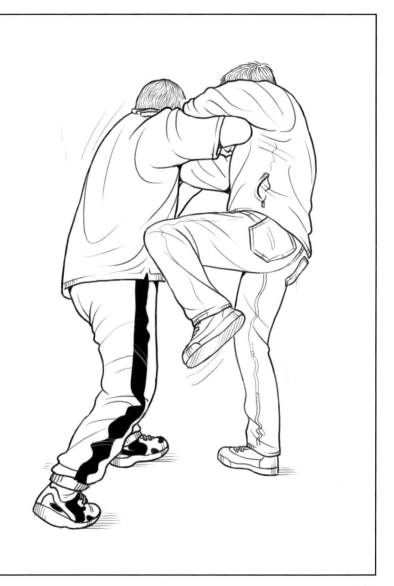

Knee to Thigh

A knee strike to the leg can be extremely effective and is hard to defend against. Loss of balance is far less likely than occurs with a body shot because the foot is off the ground for a shorter time.

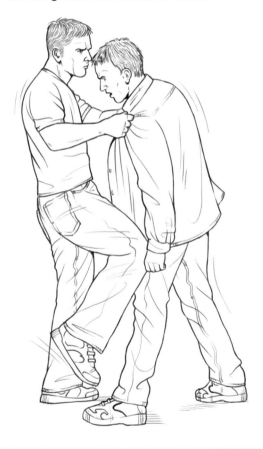

Shin Kick

A sweeping kick to the shin using the edge of the shoe causes intense pain and can put an opponent off balance. It does not require any real skill and there is little risk of being pushed over while the foot is raised.

GLOSSARY

Arrest and restraint: A body of techniques concerned with the detention of suspects by personnel involved in law enforcement or security operations. Arrest and restraint (sometimes called control and restraint) techniques are intended to cause as little harm as possible, but may rely on pain compliance to force a suspect into a controllable position.

Choke: A choke constricts the windpipe (trachea) and restricts the flow of air in and out of the body. It is accompanied by acute discomfort, which usually results in the victim struggling violently. A choke requires longer to take effect than a strangle. Choke holds are used to subdue or control an opponent. In some security applications, chokes are known by politically correct euphemisms, e.g., the 'lateral vascular restraint' replaced the 'choke hold' in some law enforcement terminology after legal complications arose from its use.

Close quarters battle: A military term for combat occurring at short range, usually in close terrain such as a defended position or an urban area. CQB is characterized by high intensity and the possibility of engagement at extremely short range, necessitating weapon-retention and hand-to-hand combat skills.

Combatives: The term 'combatives' is often applied to the general body of unarmed open-hand striking techniques used in military and law enforcement combat systems. The term is more correctly used to describe various unarmed combat systems derived from the work of W.E. Fairbairn, E.A. Sykes and Bill Underwood in the early- to mid-twentieth century.

Combato: An unarmed combative system developed by Bill Underwood in the early twentieth century for military applications.

Defendo: A less aggressive adaptation of Bill Underwood's Combato system, for use by law enforcement personnel.

Defendu: An unarmed combat system developed by W.E. Fairbairn and E.A. Sykes. Defendu began as a police system, albeit tailored to use on the streets of Shanghai in the 1930s, which was then considered the most lawless place in the world. It was later developed into a military close quarters combat system based on the same principles and taught to World War II special forces personnel.

Elbow strikes: Blows with the elbow are a staple of close-combat systems. An elbow is much less likely to be injured than a fist if it strikes something hard. Elbow strikes include hooking elbows, which follow a more or less horizontal or overhand curved path; thrusting elbows, which are driven directly to the rear or side; and rising elbows, which come up under an opponent's chin. A dropping elbow can be used against an opponent who is bent over or on the ground.

Grappling: Any situation where the combatants are able to grab hold of one another is a grappling or wrestling situation. Most unarmed fights involve at least some grappling, though skilled fighters learn to use strikes as well as grappling moves when in close combat.

Groundfighting: Any situation where the combatants are not standing upright can be considered a groundfight. Usually the fighters will try to obtain a dominant position, i.e., they are above their opponent with weight bearing down, and then either disengage or end the fight from this position. A situation where one combatant is down and others are stamping on him is not really a groundfight, though groundfighting skills can be used to escape and regain an upright position.

Hammerfists: This is a blow with the base of the fist, following an inward, outward or downward curving path. A tight fist is better protected in this position against damage than when striking with the knuckles. A hammerfist is a far more effective striking tool than the similar backfist, whereby the knuckles are used to strike.

Hand-to-hand: Hand-to-hand combat occurs when combatants are close enough to strike or grapple one another. Firearms may be used at extremely close range, but more often than not it is difficult to shoot against an enemy who is pressing in, or in the midst of a melee where there is a risk of hitting friendlies or non-combatants. Firearms may be used as hand-to-hand weapons by striking with the butt, stabbing with an attached bayonet or blocking an enemy's strike.

Haymaker: A wild, swinging punch. Untrained fighters generally throw haymakers, which are relatively easy to defend against but dangerous if they land.

Improvised weapon: Any object that is not intended for use as a weapon, but which is pressed into service as one. Sharp objects can be used to slash and/or stab, and are dealt with using the same techniques as knives. Many blunt objects are analogous to sticks or batons and are defended against in the same way. Heavier blunt instruments tend to be clumsy but can be thrown a short distance or lifted overhead and brought down on the target.

Kicks: Any strike with the foot or lower leg can be termed a kick. Kicks are rarely used in military unarmed combat, other than to finish off a downed opponent. A front kick comes directly out forwards and may be used to kick open a door. A side kick or thrust kick is directed to the side or downwards, and is similar to a stomping action used against a downed hostile. A roundhouse kick is a rotating kick normally thrown from the rear leg and impacts with the shin or instep.

Knee strikes: Any blow with the knee is termed a knee strike. A straight knee is usually delivered to the legs or body and can be used to assist an arrest and restraint technique by weakening the subject's leg. A roundhouse knee follows a similar path to a roundhouse kick, and is often used against the opponent's ribs or abdomen. A knee drop is a movement whereby the attacker simply allows his knee to buckle, dropping it onto a downed opponent with his whole body weight behind it.

Krav Maga: An Israeli combat system developed for police and military applications. Krav Maga has become a popular martial art and has spawned several variants. Some are more effective in combat than others, though this is more due to training methodology than the content.

Martial Arts: Originally a term for fighting and combat systems, the meaning has drifted over the years to include a range of activities, of which some are only peripherally connected with combat. Some martial arts are combat effective; others are over-stylized or might better be described as sports and/or fitness classes.

Milling: Some military forces use milling to develop fighting spirit. Although milling is in some ways similar to sparring it is not really about fighting skills, as the aim is to be extremely aggressive without regard to defense.

Modern street combat: a self-defense system developed by Dave Turton from various sources, including the Western martial arts and military unarmed combat systems. It is currently taught by the author and other instructors within the Self-Defence Federation.

Officer safety: A law enforcement term for a body of technique designed to help officers avoid injury. Some techniques are physical and can also be used for arrest and restraint. Others, such as threat assessment, are non-physical but will shape the officer's response to a situation.

Punch, hooked: Hooked punches can be thrown with the lead or rear hand, and strike with the knuckles of a closed fist. A forward body punch, sometimes called a shovel hook, and an uppercut, a rising punch that lands under the chin, can also be considered to be hook punches. The wild haymaker is essentially a poorly executed hook targeted at the head.

Punch, straight: Straight punches with the knuckles of a closed fist include the jab, which is a fast, light strike used mainly in boxing and similar competitions; the lead straight, which is similar but lands with much more force; and the cross, which is a very powerful blow delivered from the rear hand.

Rolling: Freeform groundfighting (sometimes starting from an upright position and going to the ground via a takedown) is termed rolling. Rolling can be intensely competitive or used as a medium for skills practice. It is used to build confidence and fighting spirit along with developing groundfighting skills.

GLOSSARY

Self-defense: The act of physically repelling an assault. Self-defence is a subset of self-protection.

Self-protection: The whole range of measures that might be taken to ensure a person's own safety. These include physical measures (self-defense) but also skills such as conflict management, threat awareness and threat-avoidance techniques.

Sidearm: A relatively small, easy-to-carry weapon is termed a sidearm. Historically this includes various types of sword and dagger, but in the modern context it normally refers to a handgun or small submachine gun. Sidearms are normally carried in a shoulder or belt holster and can be relatively easily concealed.

Sparring: Sparring is freeform striking with a partner. The degree of contact and the focus can vary; sparring can be a technical exercise or a test of fighting spirit and endurance. Sparring differs from 'real' combat but it is still a useful training method.

Strangle: A strangle cuts off the blood supply to the brain, resulting in rapid unconsciousness and, if kept in place, death. A firmly placed strangle can cause unconsciousness in a few seconds; strangles used for this purpose are sometimes termed 'sleeper holds'. Many strangles also at least partially cut off the windpipe, and are thus combinations of a strangle and a choke.

Takedown: A takedown is a technique designed to make an opponent fall or to drive him into the ground. Precisely defined, a takedown does not involve lifting the opponent's weight.

Throw: Throws are less commonly used in military combat systems as they are harder to execute. They do cause more damage, however. A throw involves lifting the opponent's weight momentarily, then causing him to fall to the ground.

Weapon retention: A body of techniques based around keeping control of a weapon in a close-quarters fight. Creating space to use the weapon is an important secondary consideration.

INDEX